Jesus
THE HEART OF THE MATTER

THE MASTER'S MANIFESTO
ON WHAT MATTERS MOST

DR. DORAL R. PULLEY

No part of this book may be reproduced or transmitted in any form or by any means, electronic or mechanical, including photocopying and recording, or by any information storage retrieval system, except as may be expressly permitted in writing by the publisher. Request for permission should be addressed in writing to **COTEK Press**, Attn: Dr. Doral R. Pulley at the following address:
2119 Gwynn Oak Avenue, Baltimore, MD 21207

ISBN #0-9719941-4-5 | 978-0-9719941-4-0

© *2021 Printed in the United States of America*

Table of Contents

Dedication 6
Acknowledgments 7

Introduction 8
Heart of the Matter Chart 10
Setting the Stage 12

Week 1 17
Week 2 29
Week 3 41
Week 4 53
Week 5 65
Week 6 77
Week 7 88

Conclusion 99
Resources 103

Dedication

I dedicate this book to my aunt, **Minister Chiquita Blake Park Moses** (March 19, 1958 – December 27, 2020), who made her transition while I was writing this devotional. Aunt Chee Chee, as I affectionately called her, was the matriarch of our family, a wife, a mother, a grandmother, an aunt, a great aunt, a spiritual sister, a friend, and a church member. She loved arts, travel, and nature. Her spirituality was evident in how she showed up in her life. I know that she did not die because there is no death in reality. "She that lives and believes in me will never die (John 11:26)." I know that she did not pass away because her memory will never pass away from our hearts (I Thessalonians 4:13). I know that we did not lose her because we know where she is. "To be absent from the body is to be present with the Lord (2 Corinthians 5:8)." We release her from this dimension of life, abundant life, to the next dimension of life, eternal life (John 3:16, 10:10).

I dedicate this book to **Elder Delores Russ**, one of my spiritual godmothers, confidants and prophetic voices in my life, who transitioned just before this book was published. I AM living the fulfillment of the words that she spoke 25 years ago that my life and ministry will take off in my late 40's early 50's.

Introduction

Acknowledgments

I appreciate **Overseer Julius L. Ford**, General Secretary of the Church of the Everlasting Kingdom, Inc., for publishing this book. We have an incredible synergy that makes projects a joy to complete. These endeavors not only bless us, but they bless the earth.

I appreciate **Minister Gina L. Folk**, Today's Church Vision Leader, for "Leading with Spirit." You have been by my side every step of the way with this book – writing, rewriting, editing, synchronizing concepts, and ensuring that everything is in alignment with our doctrine. I AM so glad that we are on the same team.

My heart is full of gratitude for **Bishop A. Bernard Hector** for being the best brother and Vice Presiding Prelate this side of heaven. Your loyalty and faithfulness "down through the years" is unprecedented.

My heart is full of gratitude for **Dr. Davina Jones** for being the Assistant to the Spiritual Leader at Today's Church Tampa Bay. I can do what I do because I know that you have the local assembly covered. God has brought you to the Kingdom for such a time as this.

I AM grateful for **Elder Marilyn Schoenfelder** for editing this book and for all your positive words of affirmation throughout the process. You are indeed a blessing.

I AM grateful for the members of the Kingdom Writer's Master Class (**Bishop Teto, Bishop D. Walter, Overseer Sam, Elder Marilyn, Elder Reynaldo, Elder Cheri, Minister Gina, Minister S. Christine**) for holding the vision with me of writing every day, being a world-renown author, whose books have multiple translations.

I thank God for **Shepherd Mother Renet Dennard Cole** for being a great resource of inspiration. You always believe in me and support my visions. Your assistance with Executive Administration makes my load lighter.

Introduction: Jesus' Manifesto

This book is an in-depth study of Jesus' Sermon on the Mount as found in the Gospel of Matthew chapters 5-7. The Sermon on the Mount is Jesus' Manifesto on Matters that Matter, his Standard Operating Procedures (SOP). Most of his disciples were Jewish men who followed the Law and the Prophets. Once they began to follow him, he took the opportunity to take them to the mountain and teach them his Kingdom principles, practices, and promises. We break down these topics over seven weeks and cover a wide variety of matters to empower us to be Jesus' disciples today.

The Consciousness Journey

The Consciousness Journey is a 7-Week process that typically happens during the Lenten Season; however, it can be effective any time during the year that you desire to make a significant change in your life and relationship with the Divine.

Each February, the National Heart, Lung, and Blood Institute (NHLBI) marks American Heart Month by raising awareness about heart health and urging Americans to reduce their risk factors for developing cardiovascular disease. Each week of the Lenten Season Consecration, we will focus on heart health both physically and metaphysically through various activities.

At the beginning of each week:

1. We focus on our *physical heart* with:
    a. **Digestion** by eating **a lot of, a little of,** and **avoiding** certain foods. We maintain or improve excellent heart health based on the foods and beverages that we consume. Be sure to consult your physician or dietitian before making changes to your regular eating routines, especially those who experience God in the form of medication.
    b. **Self-Care Strategy** to improve our heart health. We will focus on one of Pulley's 8 Self Care Strategies.
    c. **Prayer.** We will pray and hold the consciousness for healing from a particular heart disease through focused prayer.

Introduction

2. We focus on our *metaphysical heart* through:

    a. **Feeling.** By examining a feeling that adversely impacts our holistic growth and development.

    b. **Healing.** By focusing on a **Kingdom Practice for the Development of the Soul** to heal our metaphysical heart from the featured feeling.

During the week:

Each day we will read about a Matter from the Master's Manifesto in Matthew 5-7. We encourage you to create or join a support group to help you through the process.

At the end of each week:

1. We will read about a Mountaintop Experience that the author had relating to one of the Matters that the Master, Jesus Christ, taught and the underlying Kingdom Principle for Divine Living.

2. You will also have an opportunity to write about your Mountaintop Experience relating to one of the Matters that the Matter that we read during the week.

Heart of the Matter Chart

Week	A Lot	A Little	Avoid	Self-Care Strategy
1	Water	Tea and Coffee	Alcohol, Sodas and Dairy	Intimacy
2	12 pm- 8:00 pm	8 am- 12 pm	Eating after 8 pm	Rest
3	Fresh meats and vegetables	Frozen meats and vegetables	Canned and processed meats and vegetables	Exercise
4	Raw vegetables and berries	Baked and Broiled	Fried Foods (especially chicken and French fries)	Check-ups
5	Foods without sugar or starch	Brown Sugar, Wheat Flour, Brown Rice	White Sugar, White Flour, White Rice	Treats
6	Meat less Meals	Turkey, Chicken and Seafood	Beef, Lamb and Pork	Outward Appearance
7	Water, raw veggies fresh fruits, nuts, lentils, beans	Flat Bread and Veggie Pasta	Pizza and Pasta	Recreation

Introduction

Metaphysical (Soul) Heart Disease	Kingdom Practice	Mountain-top Topic	Kingdom Principle
Jealousy	Scripture, Denial, and Affirmations	WayShower	Divine Purpose
Envy	Tithing of Time, Talent and Treasure	Higher Perspective	Divine Nature
Strife	Writing and Journaling	Pure Heart	Divine Provision
Bitterness	Thanksgiving, Praise and Worship	Anger	Divine Placement
Malice	Meditation, Mindfulness and Breathing	Divorce	Divine Timing
Hatred	Visioning and Visualization	Worry	Divine Protection
Slander	Fellowship with the Saints and Positive People	Golden Rule	Divine Order

Setting the Stage

Biblical Foundation for 40 Days

The number 40 is significant in the Bible. Several biblical figures did things for 40 days. Biblically, the number forty (40) represents probation or a time of testing. Forty days was a prominent time frame in the life of Moses and the children of Israel. Moses was on Mt. Sinai receiving the Law for 40 days and 40 nights (Exodus 24:18). This period was a time of fasting and consecration for him. Like Moses, you will ascend for the next 40 days to a higher state of consciousness through consecration. Moses went back to Mt. Sinai for another 40 days and 40 nights to pray for the children of Israel (Deuteronomy 9:18, 25).

Forty days is not just a consecration time, but it is also a time to pray with others and agree with them for their highest good. The Israelite spies took 40 days to spy out the land of Canaan (Numbers 13:25). Forty days is also a good time for us to investigate a relationship or a situation and gather all the necessary data before we decide to move forward with it.

Several biblical figures had a 40-Day experience. For example, Noah was in the flood for 40 days and 40 nights (Genesis 7:12). Therefore, Noah shows us that it may take 40 days to wash out our old thought, speech, and behavior patterns. Goliath taunted Israel's armies for 40 days before David defeated him with the slingshot and the smooth stones (I Samuel 17:16). David shows us that it may take 40 days of consistent negative results before we tire of a situation and feel ready to open our minds to do something about it.

Elijah, the prophet, stayed in Mt. Horeb for 40 days and rested after fleeing from Jezebel (I Kings 19:8). Elijah shows us that we may need 40 days to rest and reflect before making our next move or beginning our next assignment. Ezekiel, the prophet, laid on his right side for 40 days to represent Israel's children wandering in the wilderness for 40 years (Ezekiel 4:6). Ezekiel shows us that it may take us 40 days of demonstration before we really get the point.

Forty days was also significant in the life and ministry of Jesus. Jesus was in the wilderness for 40 days and 40 nights fasting and praying (Matthew 4:2). Like Jesus, we are entering into a time of consecration and fasting for 40 days so that we will be empowered and equipped to do what God called us to do. Jesus was seen of his disciples 40 days before he ascended back

Introduction

into heaven (Acts 1:3). Like the disciples, it may take us 40 days to release our old vision of Jesus and see him in a new way.

Biblical Foundation for Fasting

Praying and fasting are powerful, spiritual practices that help us develop as disciples. Jesus fasted, and he taught his disciples to fast as well (Matthew 6:16-18). Paul, an apostle of Jesus Christ, also reinforced the principles of fasting in his epistles to the local assemblies by telling them that they are to be "in fastings often (II Corinthians 11:27)."

There are several different types of fasts in the Bible. One variation is the absolute fast in which Moses (Exodus 34:28-34) and Jesus (Luke 4:1-13) were set apart for 40 days without food or water. Some fasts were for shorter periods, such as the three days and three nights that Esther did with her maids (Esther 4:1-5:5) or as Jonah did in the belly of the great fish (Jonah 3:1-10). Other fasts called for people to abstain from particular foods and drinks for an extended period, as Daniel and the three Hebrew boys did (Daniel 10:1-21). The fast suggested in this devotional resembles Daniel's fast.

Consecration is more than abstaining from certain foods or attempting to release weight. Consecration is a time to focus and concentrate on our holistic growth and development. Although there are 49 days of readings, the fasting portion of this consecration is 40 days beginning Ash Wednesday and ending Good Friday. Sundays are also free days to take a break from dietary restrictions and prepare for the new week's challenge. Each of us has a choice to simply focus on the fasting requirements for the week or to progressively build upon each week, adding an additional requirements.

Pulley's 8 Self-Care Strategies – D.I.R.E.C.T.O.R.

1. Digestion (the foods and beverages we consume) Romans 14:2-4

2. Intimacy (knowing and being known) Ecclesiastes 4:8-10

3. Rest (getting the sleep we need to function at our optimal) – Psalm 127:2

4. Exercise (physical movement, activity) – I Timothy 4:8

5. Check-ups (going to doctors and dentists) Jeremiah 8:21-22, Matthew 9:12

6. Treat Yourself (rewarding ourselves for our progress) Ecclesiastes 9:7

7. Outward Appearance (hygiene and looking our best) I Samuel 16:7, Matthew 5:16

8. Relax (having fun, entertainment, vacations) Proverbs 17:22

Introduction

The 12 Kingdom Practices for the Development of the Soul

1. Reading, Studying and Researching the Scriptures – II Timothy 2:15
2. Quoting Scriptures, Denials and Affirmations – Matthew 16:19
3. Thanksgiving, Praise and Worship – John 4:24
4. Fasting and Forgiving – Isaiah 58:1-10
5. Stillness and Movement – Psalm 46:10
6. Silence and Sound – Habakkuk 2:20
7. Giving and Stewardship of Your Time, Talents and Treasure – Galatians 6:6-10
8. Fellowship with the Saints and Positive People – Acts 2:41-47
9. Visioning and Visualization – Habakkuk 2:1-4
10. Meditation, Mindfulness, and Breathing – Joshua 1:1-8
11. Writing and Journaling – Revelation 1:19
12. Witnessing and Sharing Your Testimony with Others – Psalm 105:1

Kingdom Principles for Divine Living

THE KINGDOM PRINCIPLE OF DIVINE NATURE We believe the nature of God is love. We love God, ourselves, and everyone else. Who we are is Divine, created in the image and likeness of God (Matthew 22:34-40, John 10:30, Romans 8:38-39, Psalms 84:11).

THE KINGDOM PRINCIPLE OF DIVINE PURPOSE We believe that the general Divine purpose for all life is to conform to the image of the Christ consciousness. Every being is also born with a Divine specific purpose, our why, to be discovered and fulfilled (John 10:10, Romans 8:28-29, I Corinthians 12:3-14, Galatians 5:22-23, Ephesians 4:11- 16, Romans 14:17, Luke 17:20-21).

THE KINGDOM PRINCIPLE OF DIVINE ORDER There is a Divine Order in the universe, and everything that happens in this life is according to that Divine Order (Psalms 37:23, Galatians 6:6-10).

THE KINGDOM PRINCIPLE OF DIVINE TIMING There is a Divine Timing in the universe and that everything happens according to that Divine Timing (I Peter 5:6, Esther 4:14, Matthew 6:28-33).

THE KINGDOM PRINCIPLE OF DIVINE PLACEMENT There is a Divine Placement in the universe. We are precisely where we are supposed to be spiritually, mentally, emotionally, physically, geographically, financially, educationally, vocationally, relationally, and socially (Philippians 4:11, I Timothy 6:6).

THE KINGDOM PRINCIPLE OF DIVINE PROVISION God has already provided everything that we need naturally and spiritually. We believe that God is our Source of perfect health, wealth, and harmony in all relationships (II Peter 1:3- 4, Psalms 23, Psalms 37:4, Philippians 4:19, Luke 6:38).

THE KINGDOM PRINCIPLE OF DIVINE PROTECTION God divinely protects and encompasses us with a hedge of protection. Anything that gets through that hedge of protection to us was meant to be and intended for God's glory and our good (Psalms 34:7, Job 1:10, II Timothy 1:7, Isaiah 54:17, Hebrews 13:6, Psalms 27:1-2)

Week One

Introduction: Jesus' Life Events Leading to the Sermon on the Mount

Jesus of Nazareth lived 33 years in his physical body. He accomplished a lot during that time frame, including and not limited to preaching, teaching, healing, developing disciples, training church leaders, and performing miracles, signs, and wonders.

Jesus was a Master Teacher and a powerful Wayshower to his disciples, the multitudes that followed him, individuals who experienced miracles through their interactions with him and his day's religious leaders. The Gospels illustrate Jesus' example of successfully navigating through the nine phases of life: pre-existence with God, birth, life, ministry, death, burial, resurrection, ascension/intercession, and Second Coming. This week, to prepare us for the Sermon on the Mount, we will follow Jesus' major life events leading up to the Sermon on the Mount. Bear in mind that following Jesus as a Wayshower empowers you to be a Wayshower for others throughout your life cycle.

This Week's Work at a Glance

The Physical Heart

1. *Digestion – focus on the beverages that you consume.*

    A Lot – Water

    A Little – Coffee, Tea

    Avoid – Alcohol, Sodas, and Dairy

2. *Self-Care Strategy – Intimacy*

    Intimacy is knowing and being known. Let a close family member, friend, or church member know your thoughts and feelings about the lifestyle change you choose to make during this Consciousness Journey. Also, listen to their thoughts and feelings about it as well. Invite them to journey with you in whatever way resonates with each of you.

3. *Collective Consciousness Prayer for Healing of Heart Attacks*

   Condition: A heart attack is when the heart stops beating suddenly. This week, pray the prayer below and hold the consciousness of healing of heart attacks.

   Prayer: Beloved, I wish all things that you prosper and be in health even as your soul prospers (3 John 1:2). We hold the consciousness of healing, health, and wholeness for those who experienced heart attacks, those impacted by a person who has had a heart attack, and those at risk of heart attacks. It is in the name and through the power and in the consciousness of Christ Jesus that it is so, so it is, and so we let it be.

The Metaphysical Heart

4. *Heart Issue: Jealousy*

   Jealousy is when you want to be someone else. You feel that another person is better than you. Jealousy is a heart issue that causes you to experience low self-esteem, lack of self-worth, and poor self-image.

5. *Kingdom Practice for the Development of the Soul: Scripture, Denials and Affirmations*

   Work to overcome jealousy with the spiritual tool of Scripture, denials, and affirmations. Imagine a hammer. Quoting Scripture is the handle, the Universal Truth. Denials are the claw pulling up old ideas and limiting beliefs that are firmly planted and nailed into your consciousness. Affirmations are the head that securely fastens the good desires of your heart. Heal your heart and hammer out jealousy with the Scripture, denial, and affirmation listed below.

   Scripture: "Love is strong as death; jealousy is as cruel as the grave (Song of Songs 8:6)."

   Denial: I release and let go of jealousy. I do not need to be jealous of anyone.

   Affirmation: We are all one. I AM one with God. I AM with all life. I AM one with One.

The Master's Manifesto

6. *Readings for the Week*

    Read about Jesus' life cycle in Matthew 1-4 and Luke 2

7. *Matters that Matter*

    This week's daily topics: Jesus' birth, early life, baptism, message, wilderness, choosing disciples, and traveling miracles.

Day 1 – Birth

"And knew her not till she had brought forth her firstborn son: and he called his name Jesus (Matthew 1:25)."

Jesus was not born under ideal circumstances. His conception was Immaculate, yet very few people believed it. Many people thought that Joseph and Mary consummated their marriage before the honeymoon. Others thought Mary was unfaithful to her fiancé, Joseph, and Jesus was the result of her infidelity. Joseph even considered calling off the wedding until an angel appeared to him in a dream, informing him that Jesus was not conceived out of wedlock but by the Holy Ghost. In each scenario, people depicted a dark cloud around the circumstances of Jesus' conception.

Whether your parents were married, separated, or divorced, your conception was perfect for your purpose. Maybe your parents were unmarried teenagers or adults who had not planned on having any more children; your conception was still divine. Even if you were the product of rape, incest, abuse, or adultery, your conception was still divine. The principle of Divine Order surrounded your presence. As challenging as it may be to grasp, the **Kingdom Principle of Divine Order** reminds you of the truth that everything that has happened in your life happened exactly how it was supposed to happen. Your conception is no exception.

There are no accidents. There are no coincidences. There are no mistakes. Therefore, you have no reason to feel ashamed. There is no reason to hold your head down about the circumstances that brought you to this planet. Like Jesus, you can show people that you can live a happy, healthy, prosperous, and successful life regardless of your birth circumstances.

_____

_____

_____

_____

_____

_____

_____

Day 2 – Early Life

"And he said unto them, how is it that you sought me? Don't you understand that I must be about my Father's business (Luke 2:39)?"

The spiritual awakening that Jesus had at 12 years old was only for him. It was not for Mary, Joseph, or the public. His experience was for him to awaken to the truth of who he was and what God called him to do. The scriptures do not record him doing any public ministry for another 18 years after his awakening. During these years, he went back home, submitted to his parents, and continued to grow (Luke 2:39-52).

Some insights that you receive are not for immediate implementation. God gave them to you so that you can build consciousness and confidence around those ideas. You do not need to share everything God shares with you with everyone else. Sometimes the only thing that Spirit intends and asks you to do is submit to a process. Often, that submission process includes writing things down and sitting with the information until the right and perfect time to bring it into physical manifestation.

Be patient with yourself and submit to your process. Salvation is not a one-time experience. It is a constant unfolding of your consciousness. You may fall asleep and need to wake up more than once before you actualize the fullness of your spiritual identity. There may be several alarm clocks that sound before you are sure of your calling (2 Peter 1:10). Even after you are sure of who you are, there will be times when you need a reminder that you are a unique, unrepeatable expression of God.

_____
_____
_____
_____
_____
_____
_____
_____
_____

Day 3 – Baptism

"I indeed baptize you with water unto repentance. but he that cometh after me is mightier than I, whose shoes I am not worthy to bear he shall baptize you with the Holy Ghost, and with fire (Matthew 3:11)."

Jesus went to the Jordan River with the full intention of being baptized by John the Baptist. Once he made up in his mind that he would live a new life filled with ministry and miracles, he washed away his old life through the waters of baptism. When approached, John did not feel worthy to baptize Jesus. He felt Jesus should baptize him. As Wayshower, Jesus insisted that John perform the baptism. Jesus was clear that even he was not exempt from the process.

Repentance and water baptism are like soap and water; they go together. Repentance cleanses your consciousness from any error-thinking, and baptism washes those thoughts away.

Baptism is not limited to a one-time experience. You do not have to wait for a new year, birthday, anniversary, or special ceremony. You can be baptized or baptize yourself as often as you feel the need to wash away that which no longer serves you. Each day is an opportunity for you to have a new beginning and a fresh start.

Day 4 – The Message of the Kingdom

"From that time, Jesus began to preach, and to say, repent for the kingdom of heaven is at hand (Matthew 4:17)."

Kingdom is a compound word consisting of two words, king and domain. The king is the leader or the authority figure, and the domain is where the king rules and reigns. Jesus' ministry was to establish the Kingdom of God on the earth. This calling was a continuation of the message of his cousin and spiritual leader, John the Baptist (Matthew 3:1-2).

Jesus, the king of the Kingdom, was establishing God's Kingdom on the earth during a time when his people, the Jews, were under Roman oppression. The Jews invited Roman leadership to help them maintain control of their Promised Land. What began as help eventually became a hindrance. They became burdened with their tithes for the synagogue and taxes to Caesar. Their fear and confusion caused them to incorporate pagan rituals into their religious traditions, which did not change the circumstances.

They were open and receptive to finding a physical king to help them overthrow the current governmental system and empower them to reclaim their power and land. The Kingdom that Jesus was establishing was not physical; it was a spiritual kingdom. The Kingdom of God is a system, a form of government, a way of being, seeing, thinking, speaking, and behaving in which God is the center. The Kingdom that Jesus espoused is in all of us (Luke 17:20-21).

Day 5 – The Wilderness

"Then was Jesus led up of the Spirit into the wilderness to be tempted of the devil (Matthew 4:1)."

As Wayshower, Jesus was Lord of lords. He demonstrated how to be lords on the earth. Typically, when you think of the word, lord, you think about ruling, controlling, or mastering other people. Being a lord in the evolution of consciousness is being master over you. To rule yourself and your world, you must love God AND love yourself, which in turn empowers you to love others. "Better is he that rules his own spirit than he that takes a city (Proverbs 16:32)." Being lord is not about controlling others through manipulation, domination and arrogance. Being lord is not thinking and feeling that you know what is best for others. As demonstrated by Jesus Christ, Lord is about controlling your passions, one of the aspects of the fruit of the Spirit (Galatians 5:22-23). It is about ruling over your soul.

After Jesus received validation of his identity from God, the affirmation of his identity through John the Baptist, and confirmation of his mission from the dove that descended on him at his baptism, Jesus needed time to integrate all that happened before he began his ministry. He took time to be alone so that he was able to make meaning of it for himself. The wilderness was the perfect place to do that. Every Wayshower has his/her own wilderness experience.

The wilderness experience allows you to address and integrate all four aspects of your soul. Your soul is composed of your mind (thinking), your heart (feelings), your intellect (learned perceptions/processing), and your will (choosing). You know that you are ready to leave the wilderness and begin doing ministry when you have addressed all four aspects of your soul. The wilderness experience is a soulful experience that empowers you with the necessary tools to handle anything that comes up while you are doing ministry.

_____

_____

_____

_____

Day 6 – Choosing Disciples

"And they straightway left their nets and followed him (Matthew 4:20)."

The word, disciple, appears over 250 times in the King James Bible. Many strong historical figures and biblical leaders such as Moses, John the Baptist, and Jesus had disciples who committed their lives to follow them and their teachings. "The disciple is not above his master (Matthew 10:23)," but he serves the master/leader and learns his teachings. In John 9:28, several people make a declaration, "You are his disciple, but we are Moses' disciples." In Luke 7:17-19, John the Baptist sends his disciples to question whether Jesus is indeed the Messiah or should they look for another. Jesus also used the term, disciple, to refer to those who followed him closely. He distinguished his disciples from the multitudes who followed him loosely for the miracles and the food he provided (John 6:26).

The original twelve men whom Jesus selected to follow him were called "the twelve disciples." When the term, disciple, is used, many people think of the twelve disciples who were also called apostles interchangeably in the Gospels: "Simon who is called Peter, and Andrew his brother; James the son of Zebedee, and John his brother; Philip, and Bartholomew; Thomas, and Matthew the publican; James the son of Alphaeus, and Lebbaeus, whose surname was Thaddaeus Simon the Canaanite, and Judas Iscariot, who also betrayed him (Matthew 10:2-4)."

However, other men called disciples, such as Joseph of Arimathaea, also followed Jesus (Matthew 27:57). Although not officially listed as such, Mary Magdalene, Joanna, and Susanna were women disciples of Jesus (Luke 8:3, Luke 24:10). Today, we are Jesus' disciples.

Day 7 – Traveling Miracles

"And Jesus went about all Galilee, teaching in their synagogues, and preaching the gospel of the kingdom, and healing all manner of sickness and all manner of disease among the people (Matthew 4:23)."

Jesus was not stagnant. He did not remain in one place. After his baptism, wilderness experience, and disciple selection, Jesus traveled to various places preaching. Jesus did not preach the Gospel of Jesus Christ. Jesus was the Gospel of Jesus Christ. Jesus preached the Gospel of the Kingdom (Matthew 4:22-23).

The Gospel of the Kingdom that Jesus preached was so powerful that he manifested miracles, demonstrated signs, and brought wonders into expression. The miracles Jesus manifested were healing the sick, raising the dead, casting out devils (negative influences), and cleansing the lepers. These miracles made a difference in people's lives. The blind received their sight, the deaf received their hearing, and the mute received their speech. Some of the signs that Jesus demonstrated were feeding the multitudes with a boy's lunch and having leftovers, and turning water into wine at a wedding. Jesus expressed his power through the wonders of nature, such as walking on water and commanding the storms to cease.

We still preach Jesus' Gospel of the Kingdom. It awakens people to the power within, their divine unlimited potential. The Gospel of the Kingdom is the realization of the truth of who we are and whose we are (John 1:12). The Gospel of the Kingdom empowers people to live holistically, healthy, balanced, and well-rounded lives (John 10:10). The Gospel of the Kingdom teaches people that God loves them unconditionally and desires them to live happy and prosperous lives (Luke 12:32).

Week One

My Mountaintop Experience - Jesus as Wayshower (Way-Show-Er)

Growing up in the Pentecostal Church, we focused on three phases of Jesus' existence: his death, burial, and resurrection. Sunday School classes, Bible Study, and weekly services highlighted the idea of Jesus saving us from our sins and trying to live without sin. After "getting saved," I watched people come to the altar week after week, trapped in the cycle of "sin and death (Romans 8:1-2)." They lived full of guilt, shame, and condemnation, which impacted their self-image, self-esteem, and self-worth, which in turn spread to their health, relationships, and finances.

When I went to Morgan State University, I pursued a bachelor's degree in Religious Studies and Theology. The professors emphasized Jesus' Full Life Cycle, which included his pre-existence with God, birth, life, ministry, death, burial, resurrection, ascension/intercession, and Second Coming. This formalized instruction set the tone for me to have a mountaintop experience where I realized that Jesus was more than just my Lord and Savior, he is my Christ, my King of kings, my Lord of lords, and my God manifested in the flesh. The one word that encapsulated all those titles of power and positions of authority is Wayshower. Jesus' purpose was to be a Wayshower to all humanity.

Wayshower means that Jesus is our example of what it means to be fully human and fully divine. He is the perfect balance between humanity and divinity. Wayshower means that he shows us how to think so we can have his mind and think his thoughts (I Corinthians 2:16). We can think positive thoughts and bring those thoughts into reality. Wayshower means that he shows us how to speak and say his words (John 6:63). We co-create with God the life that we desire and deserve by speaking those things that be not as though they were until they are (Romans 4:17). Wayshower means that Jesus shows us the way to act and what to do so that we can do his works and even greater works (John 14:12).

Through Jesus, my Wayshower, I began learning how to live a holistically healthy, balanced, and well-rounded life. Since my Wayshower demonstrated what it is like to live a full life, I started moving from just surviving to thriving. With this Wayshower understanding, the Holy Spirit whispered to me that my One Word was Kingdom. My purpose is developing people and leading entities through preaching, teaching, and writing about Kingdom.

Your Mountaintop Experience

In the space below, describe how Jesus is your Wayshower. How can you lead your life as Jesus did as it relates to your health, relationship, and wealth?

Week Two

Introduction – Interpreting the Scriptures that lead us to the Sermon on the Mount

The Bible is more than just one book. It is a compilation of 66 books. Due to the historical nature of the scriptures, they must be read, studied, and researched. The Old Testament lays a foundation for the New Testament. The original language of the scriptures was Hebrew, Greek, and Aramaic. The King James Version that many cherish is a translation from these original languages to Latin and English. The Bible that we read today is not the inspired Word of God. It is a translation of the Word received into a language that we can understand. We can choose to use whichever Bible translation that resonates with us as long as we preserve the original meaning.

Many scriptures parallel with others. As a student of truth, it is essential to compare scriptures to one another. To get their full understanding, strive to study both the history and context of the scriptures. *"And Jesus answering said unto them, do you not, therefore, err, because you know not the scriptures, neither the power of God (Mark 12:24)?"* The scriptures are often misunderstood and taken out of context. These misinterpretations cause confusion and sow discord. Many people use Scripture to put people into unnecessary bondage. Because of this, many individuals abandon the Bible and refuse to read or even reference it.

Here are some helpful hints to guide you to interpret Scripture correctly. Never isolate a verse of Scripture; always put it in the chapter's context and the book in which it resides. Whenever you read a passage, ask the following questions: Whose speaking? To whom is the author speaking? What is the character saying, and why? How does this verse apply to my life?

Remember, everyone does not look at the Bible the same way. Some people take it literally and see it as the inherent infallible Word of God. Other people see it as literature and provide literary criticism about the accuracy of various events and characters. Finally, others read the scriptures for life-application and focus on the principles and practices that help them make their lives better and more fulfilled.

This week we will take Matthew 5:1-2 line by line and precept upon precept to better understand the setting from which Jesus gave the Sermon on the Mount (Isaiah 28:19).

Jesus: The Heart of the Matter

This Week's Work at a Glance

Physical Heart

1. *Digestion*

    Avoid – Eating after 8:00 pm

    A Little – In the morning when you wake up, 8 am to 12 pm

    A Lot – From 12 pm – 8:00 pm (major meals)

2. *Self-Care Strategy – Rest*

    Rest in the form of sleep is essential to your physical, mental, and emotional health. When you get proper rest, your body recalibrates itself. When you do not get the right amount of sleep, you can be lethargic, mentally drained, and emotionally edgy. Only you know exactly how much rest you need to function at your optimum. Whatever that is, give that gift to yourself. Also, remember naps are great during the day to rejuvenate yourself.

3. *Collective Consciousness Prayer for Healing Heart Failure*

    Condition: Heart Failure occurs when a heart muscle becomes weak or stiff and fails to expand and contract as needed.

    Prayer: We are fearfully and wonderfully made. Our souls know that right well (Psalm 139:14). We speak to the hearts of all those diagnosed with heart failure and command their hearts to function according to the purpose that God made them. It is in the name and through the power and in the consciousness of Christ Jesus that it is so, so it is, and so we let it be.

Metaphysical Heart

4. *Heart Issue – Envy*

    Envy is a sibling of jealousy. Whereas jealousy is wanting to be who someone else is, envy is wanting what someone else has.

5. *Kingdom Practice for the Development of the Soul – Tithing your Time, Talent, and Treasure*

    Tithing is a recognition and appreciation of God as your Source. Jesus, our Wayshower, confirmed the idea of giving tithes with the right motives (Matthew 23:23). Tithe means one-tenth, giving 10% of your time, talents, and treasure in its most basic definition. You tithe your time by investing two hours and twenty-five minutes in prayer. You tithe your talents by volunteering in ministry and doing pro bono work. You tithe your treasure by giving cheerfully, freely and liberally, to the local assembly or ministry where you connect with the vision and mission and receive your spiritual feeding.

Master's Manifesto

6. *Readings for the Week*

   Read the introduction to the Sermon on the Mount in Matthew 5:1-2

7. *Matters that Matter*

   This week's daily topics: multitudes, mountains, plains, valleys, getting set, continued discipleship, messengers, and being blessed.

Day 8: What is a Multitude?

"Seeing the multitudes... (Matthew 5:1a)"

A multitude is a crowd of 70 or more people. Hundreds of thousands of people followed Jesus to see the next miracle he would perform, like opening the eyes of the blind, cleansing the lepers, or raising the dead. Many people were not interested in the spiritual food Jesus provided. They simply wanted another free meal. They were looking for the fishes and the loaves. When Jesus saw the multitudes with mixed motives, he moved to a different location, the mountain, to teach his faithful followers, the disciples.

Each person in the multitude represents a different thought or idea. You may not have thousands of followers on social media sites, but there are multitudes following you. You have a group of your thoughts and feelings that follow you wherever you go. Be aware of the internal crowd in your mind and your heart. Know that you have the power to dismiss them whenever you desire to go to a higher realm of reality.

Remember, it is not *your* thought until you think it. People have opinions about you and may even share suggestions about what you need to do. Until you give that idea energy, it is merely a suggestion. You get to choose ideas that you will keep and suggestions that you will dismiss. There is nothing wrong with taking a break to distinguish your thoughts from someone's suggestions. You have permission to pause and move away from your multitudes and manifest a different consciousness. It is your right to schedule a time to "Be still and know that I AM God (Psalm 46:10)."

Day 9: Mountains, Plains, and Valleys

"He went up to a Mountain... (Matthew 5:1b)"

Jesus gave his message on the mountain. Physically, a mountain is a large natural elevation of the earth's surface. Metaphysically, a mountain is a higher state of consciousness. It represents operating in the Christ consciousness, the Higher Mind, or the Super-consciousness. The mountain symbolizes the highest way of being, seeing, thinking, speaking, and behaving.

It is significant that Jesus did not give the Kingdom Manifesto, the Sermon on the Mount, in the plains. The plain is the level ground where most people live. The plain represents sense-consciousness or the conscious phase of mind. When you live in the plain, your natural senses govern what your eyes see, what your ears hear, what your nose smells, what your mouth tastes, and what your hands touch. You do not have to be limited by your natural senses. You can expand your consciousness to live in the supernatural realm, your spirit.

It is also significant that Jesus did not give his message in the valley. The valley represents a lower state of consciousness. Your valley is your subconscious. It is the receptacle of your past. Every memory of what you experience, along with the feelings associated with it, stays in your subconscious until you release it and let it go. The Spiritual Practice of Fasting and Forgiving empowers you to release your past to free you to co-create with God the life you desire and deserve. In Scripture, the valley was never a place of permanence. It is a temporary place that you walk through. "Yeah, though I walk through the valley and the shadow of death, I will fear no evil for you are with me (Psalm 23:5)."

___
___
___
___
___
___
___
___
___

Day 10: His first mountain, not his last

"And when he had sent the multitudes away, he went up into a mountain apart to pray, and when the evening was come, he was there alone (Matthew 14:23)."

Some scholars argue that the Sermon on the Mount is the Sermon on the Hill. Many believe that the "mountain" on which Jesus gave his Manifesto was a hill in northern Israel near the Korazim Plateau. I felt blessed with the opportunity to visit the place where Jesus gave this message to his disciples. It was not the highest mountain that I have ever climbed, but it was undoubtedly an elevated landmass. It was amazing how elevated in consciousness that I felt walking the grounds and seeing the Beatitudes in stone and various languages.

Whether you call it a mountain or a hill, mountains were an important part of Jesus' ministry. As in our scripture reading today, Jesus went to the mountain to pray. His transfiguration took place on a mountain (Matthew 17:1-9). Jesus performed miracles on mountains (Matthew 15:29-31). Jesus was betray by Judas on a mountain (Matthew 26:30). The crucifixion occurred on a mountain called Calvary (Luke 23:30). Jesus even ascended into heaven from a mountain, the Mount of Olives (Acts 1:9-12).

Like Jesus, you can pray, transform, perform miracles, and ascend from the mountains. You can also follow his example and be betrayed and crucified from the mountains. Whatever experience you have in your life, you can do it from an elevated place. The mountain consciousness does not cause us to be exempt from life challenges, but it empowers us to deal with them from a higher perspective.

Day 11: Get Set

"*And when he was set...* (Matthew 5:1c)"

Have you ever participated in a relay race? Or maybe you watched the 100 Yard Dash in person? Have you viewed the Olympics on television and seen the runners with that gleam of hope in their eyes, wishing to be the fastest person in the world? Can you visualize each runner in his or her lane in the proper posture? Do you remember hearing the words, "On your mark, get set, go?" If so, then you can relate to Jesus setting himself on the mountain preparing to share his Manifesto with his disciples, who would eventually share the Kingdom message with the entire earth.

To get set means to get prepared. It means to get your mind ready for what you are about to do. It is about setting an intention about what you desire to happen. Getting set is purifying your heart so that your motives are pure. Getting set is being clear about your desires. Getting set is releasing and letting go of distractions and consciously choosing what to focus your attention on.

The Kingdom Spiritual Practices for the Development of your Soul will help you get set. When you have a big task to do, try using *Stillness and Movement* and *Silence and Sound* to help you get set. If you do not feel motivated to complete one of your routine responsibilities, then *Breathing, Meditation and Mindfulness* are excellent resources to assist in getting set. Before you start a new project, utilize the powerful tool of *Scripture, Denials, and Affirmations* to let go of any fear, doubt, worry, stress, or anxiety. To maximize your life experiences and get the best results, get set.

_____
_____
_____
_____
_____
_____
_____
_____
_____

Day 12: Continued Discipleship

"*His disciples came unto him...* (Matthew 5:1d)"

Jesus, who represents the Christ unfolding in humanity, gave his Manifesto on a mountain to his disciples. Disciple comes from the word discipline. The disciples were disciplined followers of Jesus. After his wilderness experience, the disciples that he chose continued to follow him up the mountain to hear and better understand his Kingdom teachings. Even after the Sermon on the Mount, Jesus continued to teach and preach about discipleship.

The most essential characteristic of a disciple of Jesus is love. Jesus said in John 13:35, "By this shall all men know that you are my disciples if you have love for one another." Also, Jesus required that following him must be a priority for any of his disciples. A disciples' love for his master must be so strong that all other love relationships look like hate in comparison. Jesus said in Luke 14:26, "If any man come to me and hate not his father, and mother, and wife, and children, and brethren, and sisters, yea and his own life also, he cannot be my disciple." Therefore, being a disciple of Jesus requires sacrifice and the ability to forsake all other relationships and worldly possessions if necessary. Jesus said in Luke 14:33, "So likewise, whosoever of you that forsakes not all that he has, he cannot be my disciple."

Being a disciple of Jesus Christ is not limited to the 12 apostles or the 72 that Jesus sent out two by two. Disciples are still needed today to carry out the ministry and mission of Jesus Christ. No matter what title you receive in front of your name (bishop, elder, minister, deacon, etc.), you never graduate from being a disciple. No matter what position follows your name (BS, MD, Esquire, Director, CEO, President), you must realize the most important position is disciple. Do you consider yourself a disciple? Are you willing to manifest the real badge of discipleship, love? Will you share the Kingdom message with your family, friends, and folks that you meet?

_____

_____

_____

_____

_____

Day 13: Jesus, the Messenger

"And he opened his mouth and taught them saying... (Matthew 5:2)"

A messenger is a conduit through which the Holy Spirit channels the right and perfect message to a specific person. Sometimes a message is a confirmation of something that they already heard, and they need added assurance that they are making the right decisions about a matter. Other times a message is a "Wake Up Call" to those who are spiritually asleep and have not awakened to who they are or God's will for their lives.

Jesus was a messenger, and his message was the Kingdom. The Gospels of the Bible refer to Jesus as both a preacher and a teacher. "And Jesus went about all the cities and villages, teaching in their synagogues, and preaching the gospel of the Kingdom, and healing every sickness and every disease among the people (Matthew 9:35)." No matter what format of Jesus' message, miracles, signs, and wonders always followed.

Some scholars refer to Matthew 5:3-7 as the Sermon on the Mount, indicating that Jesus was preaching the Kingdom message to his disciples. They see it as a preached sermon because there are no breaks in the dialogue, and no one asked questions. Others see the same text as a collection of his teachings because he addressed many topics instead of one specific subject. Whether we preach and have a monologue or teach and have a dialogue, people need to hear God's message.

___
___
___
___
___
___
___
___
___
___

Day 14: Blessed: A State of Being

"And he opened his mouth, and taught them, saying, blessed are... (Matthew 5:2-3a)"

The word, blessed, occurs in the Scripture almost 300 times. In the Old Testament, blessed and cursed are actions of God (Deuteronomy 28). If people did what was right, then God blessed them, and good things happened. If they did what was wrong, then God cursed them, and bad things happened. In the Church, people often follow the same theology of the Old Testament. People walk around on eggshells hoping not to make God mad so that God does not curse them and their family. Many people dangle the blessings of God over people's heads to get them to conform to what they want them to do.

Jesus used the word, blessed, nine times in his Manifesto in the Sermon on the Mount. In the Kingdom that Jesus preached, blessed, and cursed are functions of your consciousness. Your thoughts, words, and actions bless you or curse you. When you think more deeply, feeling blessed is a state of being. It is not the result of God's action; it is your relationship with God through Christ Jesus is a blessing in and of itself (Ephesians 1:3). To abolish the notion of being cursed, Jesus took on the worst curse, the crucifixion, to ensure that we could no longer be cursed (Galatians 3:13).

One of the significant differences between the Church and the Kingdom is giving tithes and offerings. The Church teaches that you are cursed if you do not give your tithes and offerings (Malachi 3:8-10). The Kingdom focuses on sowing and reaping. If you sow bountifully, you reap bountifully (II Corinthians 9:6). If you sow sparingly, you reap sparingly. If you sow nothing, you reap nothing, but Kingdom citizens are never cursed. We are only blessed.

_____

_____

_____

_____

_____

_____

My Mountaintop Experience - Higher Perspective

Shortly after my twins' mom transitioned, a friend gifted me a retreat to Camp Agape. The person who gave me the gift thought it was an excellent idea for me to get away from the demands of being a single dad for a few days to spend some quality time with God.

On the second day of the retreat, I was walking, and I heard the Holy Spirit say, "Pay attention to your surroundings." I noticed the mountains, the water, the houses, the cars, and the people. Everything seemed so big. After I took it all in, the Holy Spirit said, "Climb up the mountain." I obeyed the divine instructions. It took me a while, but I made it to the top of the mountain. Then God said to me again, "Pay attention to your surroundings." I noticed the surrounding mountains, the water, the houses, the cars, and the people. From the aerial view, everything seemed so small.

Finally, God told me, *"This is how I see things. From this heavenly viewpoint, the things that you all think are so big are small to me. You make a big deal out of age, race, gender, orientation, height, weight, culture, educational level, socio-economic status, family dynamics, credit history, criminal background, etc. Do not identify yourself by any of those small things. That is not who you are. You are my offspring, and I love you. Focus on the big idea, LOVE. Love me (God). Love Yourself. Love Everyone Else."*

I came down from the mountain with opened eyes. I felt like the blind man who saw men as trees in the first stage of his healing, who later saw the men as they were (Mark 8:24,25). I felt like, for the first time that I saw myself through the eyes of God. I began to see others through this same lens of love. I started to see life from the divine perspective. Nothing ever looked the same again.

Your Mountaintop Experience – Higher Perspective

In the space below, describe a physical experience that you have had with being on a mountain, hill, airplane, hot air balloon, roller coaster, or any other physical elevation where your perspective was different from being on the ground.

Week Three

Introduction: Promises - Shall and Theirs

"For verily, I say unto you, till heaven and earth pass, one jot or one tittle shall in no wise pass from the law, till all be fulfilled (Matthew 5:18)."

The first part of the Sermon on the Mount is called the Beatitudes. The Beatitudes speak to the character and core values of the disciples of Jesus Christ. My Sunday School teacher, Elder Lynn, called "the Beatitudes the attitudes that better be in you if you desire to be like Jesus."

There are nine Beatitudes. Each of the Beatitudes has a promise attached to it, as indicated by the words shall or theirs. Seven of the Beatitudes have shall as a part of them. Shall is indicative of a promise that we can count on its fulfillment. Two of the Beatitudes have the word, theirs, in them. Theirs speaks of possession and ownership. It reminds us of our divine birthright and spiritual inheritance.

As we continue to grow in Christ consciousness, we will see the Kingdom Promises of health, harmony, and wealth manifested in our lives. We may not see immediate results, but we can be confident that God is faithful and does not lie (Numbers 23:19). The Universe is calling us to love even when we are waiting for the manifestation of our good. God is not just concerned about us waiting but also about our attitude while we wait, patience. In our patience, we possess our souls (Luke 21:19).

This Week's Work at a Glance

Physical Heart

1. *Digestion*

    A Lot - Fresh meats and raw vegetables

    A Little – Frozen meats and vegetables

    Avoid – Canned meats, lunched meats, or processed meats (hot dogs, sausages, etc.)

2. *Self-Care Strategy – Exercise*

    Exercise is vital to our health, especially our heart health. Most physicians recommend 30 minutes of exercise that elevates the heart rate at least three times a week. It is not just about burning calories. It is about giving our bodies the workout that it needs.

Other exercises, such as strength training, yoga, and stretching, are also great forms of exercise.

3. *Collective Consciousness Prayer for the Healing of Arrhythmia*

Condition - Arrhythmia is when the heart beats too fast, too slow, or is irregular.

Prayer - Our bodies are the temple of the Holy Spirit (I Corinthians 6:19). We release and let go of arrhythmia, and we see our hearts beating at the right and perfect time, not too fast, not too slow, and without any irregularities. It is in the name and through the power and in the consciousness of Christ Jesus that it is so, so it is, and so we let it be.

Metaphysical Heart

4. *Heart Issue – Strife*

Strife is doing anything necessary to get what you want, even at the expense of others. Strife can manifest as prioritizing work over quality time with family. It may also show up in friendships as gossip, backstabbing, and being two-faced. At its extreme, strife includes lying, stealing, violence, crime, and even murder.

5. *Kingdom Practice for the Development of the Soul – Writing and Journaling*

Work to overcome strife through the spiritual practices of writing and journaling. Write down your long-term goals for your life in addition to the short-term goals you desire to accomplish. Break down large projects into smaller bite-size pieces. Writing allows you to review your progress. Documentation empowers you to see how far you have come and how far you still must go. Like the Spirit told John on the Isle of Patmos, write (Revelation 1:19). Write your dreams and your visions. Write the whispers that you hear from the Holy Spirit and the creative ideas you receive throughout your day. Journal away your fears and frustrations by getting them out of your head and onto paper. Instead of striving for them, allow God to flow through you to bring your aspirations to pass.

Week Three

Master's Manifesto

6. *Readings for the Week*

   Read the Beatitudes found in Matthew 5:3-9

7. *Matters that Matter*

   This week's topics: openness to spirit, mourning, meekness, righteous hunger and thirst, mercy, pure hearts, and peace.

Day 15: Openness

"Blessed are the poor in spirit: for theirs is the kingdom of heaven (Matthew 5:3)."

God is Spirit, completely divine (John 4:24). Spirit does not have flesh and bones (I Corinthians 15:50). Spirit transcends time and space. Because we are God's beloved offspring, we are spiritual beings. Just as God is a threefold being: Father, Son, Holy Spirit or Mind, Idea, and Expression, we, made in the image and likeness of God, are spirit, soul, and body. The I AM is the spiritual part of our being. As spiritual beings, we can live in the Spirit, manifest the Fruit of the Spirit, and operate in the Gifts of the Spirit. (Galatians 5:17-23, I Corinthians 12:1-9).

We are spirits. We have souls. We live in bodies. Our spirit is our true identity. Our soul is composed of our minds (thinking), emotions (feeling), intellect (learning/learned perceptions) and will (choosing). Our body is the house or outer shell that houses the spirit and the soul. When we worship God, we do it from the I AM of our being and in the truth of who we are—spiritual beings.

To be poor in spirit means to be open to Spirit and to be led by Spirit, the still small voice (Romans 8:14). To be poor in spirit means that we keep our egos in check and never allow ourselves to become so haughty that we think we have arrived (Philippians 3:12-13). To be poor in Spirit means that we are always open, willing to learn, grow, unfold, heal, and develop in Christ consciousness.

Day 16: Mourning

"*Blessed are they that mourn for they shall be comforted (Matthew 5:4).*"

Loss is a normal part of the human experience from the womb to the tomb. As a baby, you lose the need for diapers and bottles. As a child, you lost teeth. Every day your body loses skin cells. Perhaps you have experienced the loss of a job, relationship, or possession.

When you lose things in your life, there are feelings attached to those losses. Some of those feelings are denial, anger, and sadness. How you deal with your feelings associated with loss is called mourning. Permit yourself to go through the grieving process. It is natural to cry when you experience a loss. Jesus, our Wayshower, cried when his friend Lazarus transitioned (John 11:35). Even though he knew the truth that he was going to raise Lazarus from the dead eventually, Jesus permitted himself to mourn (John 11:25). Jesus gave and received comfort from Lazarus' sisters, Mary and Martha.

Your divine nature seeks to comfort your soul amid sorrow. Whenever you focus on God's love and allow people to love you during the challenging times of transition, you will be comforted, as Jesus promised. The more that you choose to focus on God's love, the more comfort you will experience. God's pure love always gives you comfort. That is how you reign over the feeling of loss in your life.

Day 17: Meekness - Power Under Control

"Blessed are the meek: for they shall inherit the earth (Matthew 5:5)."

Titles of authority can cause people to be self-absorbed and ego-driven. Positions of power can stimulate unhealthy pride and delusions of grandeur. Educational degrees and societal accolades can cause people to think that they are better than others. Meekness is a power that is under the control of love (Romans 12:16). Despite titles, positions, and degrees, Jesus calls his disciples to operate in love for and consideration of other people.

When we follow Jesus' example, we can see ourselves as one with others instead of separate and apart from them. We can put ourselves in the shoes of others and treat them the way that we desire to be treated (Luke 6:31). Meekness is a healthy balance between power and love. Too much power without love causes us to be haughty and high minded. "Pride goes before destruction and a haughty spirit before a fall (Proverbs 16:18)." Too much love without power causes us to be taken advantage of, used, and abused.

We must operate from the I AM of our being and manifest the meekness that we are. Meekness is not weakness. It is a conscious choice not to manipulate, dominate, or control another person. Jesus attached a promise to being meek. He said that the meek will inherit the earth. When we practice meekness, we draw increase, abundance, overflow, and more than enough to us like a magnet. We continue in that flow as we give God the praise, glory, and honor.

Day 18: Hunger & Thirst

"Blessed are they which do hunger and thirst after righteousness: for they shall be filled (Matthew 5:6)."

The Old Testament's prophets were often God's oracles to call people to pay attention to their ways. Jeremiah, known as the weeping prophet, called God Jehovah Tsidkenu – The Lord our righteousness (Jeremiah 23:6). He knew that people were able to make the right and perfect decisions and wise choices for their lives through right relationship with God. Isaiah, the eagle-eyed prophet, spoke out against self-righteousness and called it filthy rags (Isaiah 64:6). He knew that attempting to be righteous through human effort apart from a right relationship with God was an exhausting exercise in futility.

God is righteousness. We yearn for righteousness because God created us in the image and likeness of God (Genesis 1:26-28). Righteousness does not mean that there is no room for growth or improvement. It means that we are in right relationship with God through our Spiritual Practices for the Development of the Soul such as mindfulness and meditation, fasting and forgiving, reading and studying the scriptures, praise and worship, thanksgiving and giving of our time, talents, and treasure, fellowshipping with positive people, and sharing our testimony with others.

Through right relationship with God and ourselves, we are empowered to make the right decisions and have the right perspective, right thoughts, right words, right actions, right reactions, and right feelings, thus making us righteous. Jesus was righteous and demonstrated to his disciples how to be righteous. Disciples of Jesus Christ crave righteousness. Our desire to do what is right is so strong that Jesus called it a hunger and a thirst. When we follow his example of righteousness, we fill our hunger and quench our thirst because we too become the righteousness of God (II Corinthians 5:21).

_____
_____
_____
_____
_____
_____

Day 19: Mercy

"Blessed are the merciful: for they shall obtain mercy (Matthew 5:7)."

Many people have gone to court and asked for mercy. "I throw myself on the mercy of the court" has been the plea of many who committed misdemeanors and felonies. Mercy is when we do not receive the full consequences of our actions. Mercy is in full effect when we admit that what we did was not the highest and the best and receive a lesser sentence. We receive mercy when we confess that what we said was not right and the perfect, and we get another chance to get it right.

God is merciful and gives us fresh mercy every day (Lamentations 3:22-23). We do not need to fear punishment because we do not dot every "i" or cross every "t." God is a teacher and not a punisher (Job 36:22). God's mercy is everlasting (Psalm 100:5). It never runs out, and God never gives up on us. We must extend God's mercy to ourselves and others. When we can give mercy to ourselves, then we can give it to others. When we can forgive ourselves, then we can forgive others. When we can love ourselves the way that God loves us, then we can others more perfectly.

When we operate in ego, we desire mercy for ourselves and our loved ones but demand justice for people we feel committed offenses against us. The same mercy that we desire for ourselves, we must give it to others. Jesus calls his disciples to be full of mercy, merciful, and promises that when we sow mercy, we will reap mercy. We all need mercy.

_____
_____
_____
_____
_____
_____
_____
_____
_____
_____
_____

Day 20: Pure Heart

"Blessed are the pure in heart: for they shall see God (Matthew 5:8)."

Your heart is symbolic of your feeling nature. Feelings give you the energy to do what it is that God called you to do. They also draw your good to you and you to your good. Feelings also repel that which is not good for you. Paying attention to your feelings keeps you safe and allows you to experience Divine Protection in even greater ways. Your feelings are gifts from God. Instead of judging your feelings as right or wrong, honor, and appreciate them.

Jesus, the Wayshower, reflected the heart of God. He had a big heart and accepted all people. Jesus was open to what people were feeling; therefore, his teaching, preaching, and healing ministries were effective. He knew that his heart was God's physical heart on the earth and that Spirit worked through his feelings to help humanity.

When your soul is in alignment with your spirit, your heart becomes the heart of God. It is important that when you feel something that you deal with what you feel. Address your feelings so that you are empowered to heal your past and assist others in their healing process. Your awareness of what you are feeling in the present moment manifests genuineness and causes people to feel and experience your authenticity.

Affirm today, *"When I feel, I deal. So that I can heal and keep it real as God is revealed."* - Dr. Doral R. Pulley

Day 21: Peace

"Blessed are the peacemakers for they shall be called the children of God (Matthew 5:9)."

Peace is your divine birthright as God's offspring. God desires that you live a happy, healthy, prosperous, and peaceful life. Pay attention to the people and activities that cause you to experience peace. Also, observe the times when you feel confusion, chaos, and contention. At times, to remain in a peaceful state, you may have to remove yourself temporarily from people and situations that appear to be negative to allow yourself to regroup. In other instances, you may have to permanently disconnect from people and situations that are constant disruptions to your peace.

As Wayshower, Jesus encountered a young man who appeared to be one big ball of confusion (Mark 5:1-17). The young man often cut himself and had fits of rage. He was suicidal and made several attempts to drown and burn himself to death. While his friends and family loved him, they could no longer help him; therefore, he lived in the tombs by himself. Jesus, the Prince of Peace, had enough internal peace that he helped the young man be free from his internal chaos and discover his inner peace (Isaiah 9:6).

Peacemaker is one of the terms that the scriptures use to describe you as God's child. As a peacemaker, Spirit may call you to be the meditator in personal relationships and professional situations. Allow the peace of God, which passes all understanding to exude from your presence and to change the atmosphere around you (Philippians 4:7).

My Mountaintop Experience: Pure Heart

After being a stay-at-home single dad for two years, I decided to go to graduate school to get my Masters in Pastoral Counseling and become a Licensed Clinical Professional Counselor. One of the requirements was 3000 supervised clinical hours. While I got most of my hours at St. Frances Academy, an inner-city Catholic high school, I was still short about 1000 hours. One of my colleagues suggested a placement. She said, "They always have clients, and they always need counselors, but you are probably not going to want to go there." The placement was at the National Institute for Sexually Deviant Behaviors.

My first response was, "NO!" I did not desire to provide therapy for people who were child molesters, rapists, exhibitionists, voyeurs, and frotteurs. When I ascended to the mountain, I heard the Holy Spirit whisper, "When your heart is pure, you see God in every person, in every place, and in everything." It was not about those men and what they had done. It was about me and the condition of my heart. I could not see God in them because of what they had done to children, women, and other men.

Due to my impure heart, I labeled them as child molesters when in actuality, they were the beloved offspring of God who made a poor decision to molest children. Spirit asked me, "Have you ever made a poor decision?" They were not rapists. They were God's beloved offspring who misused their power and raped women. Spirit asked me, "Have you ever misused your God-given power?" Regardless of how society labeled them, the truth is God created them in God's image and likeness, just like me.

They were not exhibitionists. They were God's beloved offspring who made a bad choice to expose themselves to others, Spirit asked me, "Have you ever made a bad choice?" They were not voyeurs. They were spiritual beings who responded inappropriately out of their pain and violated someone else's privacy. Spirit asked me, "Have you ever responded inappropriately out of your pain?" Frotteurism was a condition that they were struggling to overcome. They were not frotteurs. They were people who were perfect, whole, and complete in spirit, just like me. Spirit asked me, "Have you ever struggled to overcome a behavior that was not the highest and the best?"

As I ascended to the mountaintop and purified my heart from judgment and prejudice, I saw God in those men. I realized that people are not their conditions, their struggles, or their past. I became keenly aware of the truth that we all are God's beloved offspring, regardless of where we have been or what we have done.

As a result of this awakening in my consciousness, I effectively ministered to those men, got my clinical hours, and became a licensed therapist. I fulfilled the **Kingdom Principle of Divine Provision.** God met all of my needs. I just had to purify my heart to receive the blessings that God had already prepared for me.

Your Mountaintop Experience

In the space below, describe a mountaintop experience that you had with having a pure heart, or one of the other topics discussed this week: openness, mourning, meekness, hunger and thirst, mercy or peace.

_____
_____
_____
_____
_____
_____
_____
_____
_____
_____
_____
_____
_____
_____
_____
_____
_____
_____
_____
_____

Week Four

Introduction – Knowing who you are determines how you deal with various situations.

When we know who we are (spiritual beings living in a spiritual universe), whose we are (made in the image and likeness of God) and that God loves us (God's beloved offspring), we can make it through anything. Jesus encouraged his disciples that they were able to make it through physical and verbal persecution because they were salt of the earth and the light of the world (Matthew 5:10-15).

Rejection is a part of the human experience. You have experienced some form of rejection in your life. Perhaps it was prevalent at a particular stage of your development: childhood, adolescence, or adulthood. Maybe the rejection was crystallized in a specific relationship with parents, siblings, teachers, classmates, colleagues, or coworkers. Possibly you were rejected because of your age, gender, race, culture, height, weight, complexion, hair color, orientation, socio-economic status, criminal background, family dynamic, or for no specific reason that you can identify.

Your ability to handle rejection determines your success in life. When you see rejection through **The Kingdom Principle of Divine Placement** you realize that you are exactly where you are supposed to be. That feeling of rejection dissipates. When you feel rejected in one area, look for the lesson or the blessing of acceptance in another area. Be aware that when one door closes, a better door opens. When one window shuts, a bigger window opens. As one relationship comes to an end, take a deep breath, learn from the experience, and anticipate something new and more extraordinary.

This Week's Work at a Glance

Physical Heart

1. *Digestion*

    A Lot – Raw vegetables and fresh berries (blueberries, strawberries, blackberries, etc.)

    A Little – Baked and broiled

    Avoid – Fried Foods (fried chicken and French fries, etc.)

2. *Self-Care Strategy – Check-ups*

   We care for ourselves by taking the time to go to the doctor and the dentist. We must prioritize our regularly scheduled appointments and annual physicals. When we are too busy to attend to our health, it is an indicator that our plates are too full, and something needs to be reduced or eliminated.

3. *Collective Consciousness Prayer for the Healing of Heart Valves*

   Condition: Challenges with any of the four valves of the heart

   Prayer: We give you praise, glory, and honor that you made us in your image and after your likeness (Genesis 1:26). Just as our souls have four parts, our hearts have four chambers. We see each heart chamber and heart valve perfect, whole, and complete. It is in the name and through the power and in the consciousness of Christ Jesus that it is so, so it is, and so we let it be.

Metaphysical Heart

4. *Heart Issue – Bitterness*

   Bitterness is holding on to the past, along with the negative energy associated with it.

5. *Kingdom Practice for the Development of the Soul – Thanksgiving, Praise, and Worship*

   Thanksgiving, praise, and worship help us let go of bitterness by channeling our energy in a positive direction. Instead of focusing on what the other person said or did that did not feel good to us, we find something good about the person and relationship for which to be **thankful**. When we focus on giving God **praise** for the lesson that we learned or the blessing we received from the experience, we are less likely to become bitter. **Worship** is about seeing our oneness with God and all of God's creation. When we pray for the person with whom we feel bitter and see our oneness with the individual, we can release bitterness from our hearts.

Master's Manifesto

6. *Readings for the Week*

    Read the continuation of Jesus' Sermon on the Mount - Matthew 5:10-22

7. *Matters that Matter*

    This week's topics: physical persecution, verbal persecution, rejoicing, salt, light, the law and the prophets, and anger.

Day 22: Physical Persecution

"Blessed are they which are persecuted for righteousness' sake: for theirs is the kingdom of heaven (Matthew 5:10)."

Jesus prepared his disciples for persecution before they experienced it. When he was preparing them for physical persecution, he was also preparing himself for it. Whatever we say to others is what we need to hear ourselves. The word is a two-edged sword; it cuts both ways (Hebrews 4:12). Jesus was preparing the disciples to take up their cross because he knew one day he was going to carry his cross (Matthew 10:38, 27:40).

The persecutors did a lot to Jesus on the cross. They nailed his hands and his feet. They pierced him in his side. They put a crown of thorns on his head. They beat him, leaving 40 stripes on his back. They gave him vinegar to drink. They sold his clothes and left him naked. They persecuted him while he was in pain. Jesus allowed them to do what they needed to do, and he did what he needed to do. Through his words and actions, it is evident that Jesus understood he needed to maintain his relationship with his Father, himself, and the ones he loved. He gave his disciples access to the Kingdom of heaven by showing them how to operate in the higher consciousness despite people taking low blows. Michelle Obama said, "when they go low, we go high."

Let us not be distracted by others' actions because we have no control over what other people choose to do. Instead, in any given situation, let us focus on what God is calling us to do and do it to the best of our ability. When we are not clear what to do, let us center ourselves in the presence of God and allow the I AM to give us direction and empowerment for the next right action.

Day 23: Verbal Persecution

"Blessed are you, when men shall revile you, and persecute you, and shall say all manner of evil against you falsely, for my sake (Matthew 5:11)."

People's words only have the power that we give them. What we say to ourselves internally is more potent than what someone else says about us externally. What we say about ourselves aloud is more powerful than any words that another person can speak. Following Jesus empowers us to speak the Word with power and authority. Jesus only spoke about himself what the Father had already said about him. As disciples of Jesus Christ, we speak what God has already spoken. I only say about myself what God has already spoken about me. "I know the plans that I have for you, says the Lord... thoughts of good and not of evil to bless you and prosper you and bring you to your expected end (Jeremiah 29:11)."

People often notice your divine destiny before you see it in yourself. How they respond to your divinity, with praise or persecution, reflects where they are in their consciousness. Some celebrate you and do everything in their power to help you cultivate your potential. Others may feel intimidated by you and attempt to avoid, tear down, or hinder your development.

We do not have to wait for someone else to prophesy to us. We can prophesy our good. We do not have to be dependent on another's affirmation. We can affirm for ourselves that we are the children of God. We do not have to rely on external resources for validation; we can validate ourselves from within.

Day 24: Rejoice

"Rejoice and be exceeding glad: for great is your reward in heaven, for so persecuted they the prophets which were before you (Matthew 5:12)."

Joy is more than a feeling of happiness about things going well in your life. Joy is the demonstration of love, even when you are experiencing persecution. To rejoice means to keep experiencing joy repeatedly. When we focus on the present moment and meet the current need, we can transform any climate to rejoicing and gladness.

Joy is inside of you. It is the Fruit of the Spirit, a part of who you are as a son/daughter of God (Galatians 5:22-23). You have complete and total access to joy at every moment of your journey. To get through the pain, hurt, disappointment, and sorrow and access joy, close your eyes and take a deep breath and connect with Spirit within. Connecting with the God within allows you to move through your pain of persecution and get in touch with joy because it shifts your attention from what you lost to what you gained.

You are a disciple of Jesus Christ, and God has a purpose for your life. God divinely protects you. There is a hedge of protection around you. Anything that gets through that hedge of protection happened for God's glory and your highest good. You cannot transition from one dimension of life to the next dimension of life until you accomplish your purpose. Regardless of other people's actions or intentions, your purpose keeps you safe and gives you a reason to rejoice during persecution.

Day 25: Salt

"You are the salt of the earth: but if the salt has lost his savor, wherewith shall it be salted? it is thenceforth good for nothing, but to be cast out, and to be trodden under foot of men (Matthew 5:13)."

In his Sermon on the Mount, Jesus, the Christ, taught his disciples who they were and how to live together as children of God. One of the metaphors that he used to identify his followers was salt. Although he did not explicitly say, "I AM the salt of the earth," he did say, "You are the salt of the earth." Jesus called them the salt of the earth because he saw himself as the salt of the earth. We can only see in others that which we are.

There are many uses of salt. Salt cleanses the body. It preserves meats. Salt flavors dishes. It melts the snow. Salt also relaxes muscles. Salt always has a purpose. There is always a reason why people use salt. Salt is never meaningless. It always has a purpose.

As the salt of the earth, there is also a purpose for our lives. Everything is in divine right order. There is always a reason that we are in a particular place, at a certain time, and with a specific person or group of people. We are there to be the salt. We cleanse negative words and actions and preserve that which is good. We add flavor to bland situations. We melt away the hardness of hearts. We to relax people who are stressed or anxious. We are the salt of the earth.

_____
_____
_____
_____
_____
_____
_____
_____
_____
_____
_____
_____

Day 26: Light

"You are the light of the world. A city that is set on a hill cannot be hid (Matthew 5:14)."

One day I was singing the song, "Walk in the light, beautiful light...come where the dewdrops of mercy shine bright...shine all around us by day and by night...Jesus, the light of the world" and the Holy Spirit whispered, "Jesus is not the light of the world." I was troubled by the Spirit's words, so I went to my Bible because I believe that Scripture always supports any principle that Spirit shares with me.

The first Scripture I read was John 9:5, where Jesus stated, "As long as I AM in the world, I AM the light of the world." For the first time, I saw the truth that he set a time limit to how long he would be the light of the world. Jesus being the light of the world, was contingent on him being in the world. Through the Sermon on the Mount, Jesus taught his disciples that everything that he was, they were. We are the current disciples of Jesus Christ, and we are the light of the world.

The second Scripture I read was Matthew 5:14-16, where Jesus stated, "You are the light of the world...let your lights so shine before people that they may see your good works and glorify your Father..." The life-changing conclusion that I came to from reading these two scriptures was that when Jesus was on the earth, he was the light of the world. Now that he is no longer here in a physical sense, I AM the light of the world (individually), and we are the lights of the world (collectively). Now when I sing that song, I sing "I AM the light of the world" and alternate with "We are the light of the world" to reflect the truth that God revealed to me.

Day 27: The Law & the Prophets

"Think not that I am come to destroy the law or the prophets: I am not come to destroy, but to fulfill (Matthew 5:17)."

During Jesus' earthly ministry, he established his kingdom, which often appeared to contradict Jewish teachings such as: stoning people who were caught in adultery, eating with unwashed hands, eating with sinners, and healing on the Sabbath. In our text, Jesus clarified his mission and his purpose. He did not come to destroy the Law or discredit the Prophets. Jesus came to fulfill the Law and the Prophets. The Law he was referencing was the Law of Moses as found in the first five books of the Bible, the Pentateuch. The Prophets were the major writers (Jeremiah, Isaiah, Daniel, and Ezekiel) and minor writers (smaller books) of the Old Testament.

"Fulfilling the Law and the Prophets" means bringing out the true intention of the author. Because Jesus knew the Father/Author intimately, he provided a better understanding of what God meant, as recorded by Moses and the other Old Testament writers. He said, "For verily I say unto you, till heaven and earth pass, one jot or one tittle shall in no wise pass from the law, till all be fulfilled (Matthew 5:18)." As disciples of Jesus Christ, we follow Jesus' view of Scripture and regard it with the same dignity and openness that he did.

The scriptures are not fairy tales. All the prophecies of the Scripture have been or will be fulfilled. God watches over God's word to perform. God is not a liar. If he said it, then he is going to do it. If he spoke it, then he will bring it to pass. This truth assures every disciple of Jesus Christ that whatever word of God spoken over our lives will come to pass. No matter how long it takes.

_____

_____

_____

_____

_____

Day 28: Anger

"But I say unto you, that whosoever is angry with his brother without a cause shall be in danger of the judgment (Matthew 5:22)."

The Law and the Prophets focused on the act of murder and the punishment for such a crime. One of the Ten Commandments is "Thou shalt not kill (Exodus 20:13)." In establishing his Kingdom, Jesus was not just concerned about killing but also about the thoughts and feelings that led to murder. Jesus understood that if we change the thoughts and feelings that lead to murder, we can reduce or eliminate the act. Jesus went beyond the surface action and saw that unresolved anger is what often leads to murder.

Jesus got to the heart of the matter (anger) and not just the matter itself (murder). Notice in our text for today, Jesus advises his disciples that is not the anger that is sinful; it is what you do with it. Paul, an apostle of Jesus Christ, confirmed that it is not a sin to be angry (Ephesians 4:26). Our emotions are gifts from God. We must use the energy of our emotions to do positive things instead of negative ones.

Our emotions are not right or wrong. They just are. Our feelings provide us with fuel to accomplish various tasks. Our emotions are not excuses to say and do things that are inappropriate and hurtful to others. As stewards of our emotions, it is up to us to use the energy from our emotions to do things for the greater good.

My Mountaintop Experience – Anger

For most of my life, I had a strained relationship with my dad. He played for a minor league basketball team and wanted me to play pro basketball. He felt that my being a preacher was a phase that I would eventually outgrow. As a child, I waited for him for hours, and he was often a no call, no show. The next time he promised to take me somewhere, I believed him again as if he had not disappointed me the time before. The responsibility of our relationship rested on my shoulders. Because he was the father, and I was the son, it was my role to call him, initiate visits, and plan our events. I was so hungry for his affirmation, affection, and attention that I fell into that trap.

My New Year's Resolution for 1995 was that I would not be in unhealthy relationships of any kind. My relationship with my father was not an exception. I made a conscious choice not to initiate contact with him. Nevertheless, if he initiated contact with me, then I would respond. Several months went by, and I did not hear from him. Through the **Kingdom Principle of Divine Placement**, I accepted that I was exactly where I was supposed to be. My father was exactly where he was supposed to be. We were exactly where we were supposed to be relationally. We were only able to be where we were. We were not able to be where we were not (Philippians 4:11).

Even though we lived in the same city, we did not communicate until the day before Father's Day. He called and asked, "What are we doing for Father's Day?" My reply was the same thing that we have been doing for the past six months, "Nothing." He was confused and did not understand. I was angry, and further explained the status of our relationship and the reason why.

The next day he came to my house to take me out for Father's Day. My ego said, "Do not go with him anywhere." My spirit said, "Let go of your anger and forgive him. That was yesterday; today is a brand-new day." At that moment, I had a mountaintop experience, and the Scripture illuminated in my consciousness. "Let not the sun go down upon your wrath (Ephesians 4:26)." I decided from that day forward to give myself a day to process my anger and forgive within 24 hours.

When our bodies are functioning properly, we get the vitamins and nutrients from our food and release the waste within a day. It is the same way with our hearts and minds. God did not create us to carry waste for more than a day. Our bodies and souls cannot handle that kind of stress and pressure. Bitterness creates sickness, pain, disease, discomfort, and dysfunction in our health. Holding on to negative energy is a sure way to damage and destroy our relationships. Unforgiveness also blocks the flow of wealth in our lives. Release your good and let it flow by processing your emotions and forgiving yourself and everyone else daily.

Your Mountaintop Experience

In the space provided below, write about your own mountaintop experience with anger or any of the other topics addressed this week: physical persecution, verbal persecution, rejoicing, salt, light, the law and the prophets.

Week Five

Introduction - Love is the Answer

Love is the Kingdom Journey of every soul. Love is always our intention and guides our way of being, seeing, thinking, speaking, and behaving. Love is the all-encompassing fruit of the Spirit. Other fruit of the Spirit (joy, peace, goodness, gentleness, patience, meekness, faith, self-control) are manifestations of love through various life challenges (Galatians 5:22-23). For example, joy is the divine enablement to being loving in the face of sadness and sorrow.

"All of the law and the prophets are fulfilled in one word, love (Romans 13:8-10)." There is only one Law: Love. We fulfill the law of love in three primary ways: love God, love yourself, and love others. This week we will focus on Jesus' teaching about love. When we love God, we worship God. When we love ourselves, we are people of our word. When we love others, we do not see them as our adversaries or seek revenge. Love also causes us to pay attention to our desires and how we move in and out of relationships.

This Week's Work at a Glance

Physical Heart

1. *Digestion*

    A Lot – Foods without sugar or starch (cauliflower rice, naturally sweetened foods)

    A Little – Brown Sugar, Wheat Flour, Brown Rice

    Avoid – White Sugar, White Flour, White Rice

2. *Self-Care Strategy* – Treats

    It is essential to treat yourself for your accomplishments and the progress that you make towards your goals. When you treat yourself, it gives you the energy to keep forging ahead. It also saves you from being dependent on the praise of others for your success. A treat can be going to a restaurant you always desired to dine in or a special gift that makes you smile. The treat does not have to be food or something that costs money. It can be as simple as a candlelit bath, walking around the park, enjoying your favorite movie, spending time on the beach, or watching the sunset. Whatever causes you to feel appreciated is a treat.

3. *Collective Consciousness Prayer for the Healing of Heart Infections*

   Condition: A Heart Infection is when the heart contracts an infection like a cold.

   Prayer: Thank you, God, that you forgive us, and you heal us from all our diseases (Psalm 103:3). We wrap our hearts in the healing light of God's love and heal any infections. It is in the name and through the power and in the consciousness of Christ Jesus that it is so, so it is, and so we let it be.

Metaphysical Heart

4. *Heart Issue:* Malice

   Malice is wanting to inflict pain or cause harm to another person.

5. *Kingdom Practice for the Development of the Soul* – Meditation, Mindfulness, and Breathing

   Meditation, mindfulness, and breathing are powerful tools that keep your soul level with your spirit. Meditation focuses on a specific idea. You go into meditation with a question and come out with an answer. Mindfulness occurs when you become aware "in the moment" of your thoughts and the feelings you experience. Mindfulness causes you to become even-tempered and at peace with whatever is going on right here and right now. Conscious breathing helps you connect with God, the breath of life that is within you. It also recalibrates the brain and rejuvenates the body. When you meditate on peace, are mindful of your thoughts and feelings "in the moment," and breathe, you can release and let go of malice.

Master's Manifesto

6. *Readings for the Week*

   Read the continuation of Jesus' Sermon on the Mount Matthew 5:23-48

7. *Matters that Matter*

   This week's topics: worship, adversaries, lust, divorce, vows, revenge, and love.

Day 29: Worship

"Leave there your gift before the altar and go your way; first be reconciled to your brother, and then come and offer your gift (Matthew 5:24)."

Most people enjoy giving and receiving gifts. When we give a person a gift, we desire to be sure that they will enjoy it and can use it. We put special effort into ensuring that it is the right style, color, and size. The better we know the person, the better we can choose the perfect gift. Our thanksgiving, praise and worship is a gift to God. Based on our relationship with God, we know what pleases God. Do not just give God anything. Find out what God desires from you and give it to God. Make sure that your gift of thanksgiving, praise and worship is acceptable to God.

Jesus described worship as bringing a gift to the altar. Now that we know that our thanksgiving, praise and worship are gifts to God, we must now discover the altar. In the Old Testament, the people erected altars in various places to remember a special event between them and God. It was also their custom to build an altar to thank God for a blessing that they received or a miracle that God performed. Today, we often think of the altar as the front of the church where people pray. However, because we are the temple of God and the Holy Spirit dwells within us, we can build an altar of thanksgiving, praise and worship anywhere at any time. We are not limited to a particular time and space. Build an altar in your home, on your job, at school, and any place that you desire to worship God. Build an altar wherever you are.

The very root of thanksgiving, praise and worship is remembering. Thanksgiving is the manifestation of appreciation of what God had done for us. We produce praise when we remember that God is our Source and everything and everyone else is a resource. Worship is the result of remembering our oneness with God and that nothing can separate us from God. Thanksgiving, praise and worship are not activities that we can enter without thinking and remembering. In preparation for thanksgiving, praise and worship, we must take time to reflect on our relationship with God, ourselves, and others.

_____
_____
_____
_____

Day 30: Adversaries

"Agree with your adversary quickly, while you are in the way with him; lest at any time the adversary deliver you to the judge, and the judge deliver you to the officer, and you be cast into prison (Matthew 5:25)."

H. Emile Cady in *Lessons in Truth* suggested that the primary cause of suffering is forgetting our divine nature. The secondary cause of suffering is our stubborn refusal to change. Once we understand why we suffer, then we can end it. God does not desire for us to suffer. God desires for us to experience the best that life has to offer. We are heirs of God and joint-heirs with Christ Jesus; therefore, Jesus entitled us to the abundant life he promised his disciples (Romans 8:17, John 10:10).

Whenever we see someone as an enemy or an adversary, we have forgotten our divine nature, and suffering begins. Enemies are the inner me. Enemies represent that part of us that we have not accepted. We are light and darkness, good and evil. All of it makes us a whole person. Just as a day is not complete unless there are evening and morning, we can not see ourselves as complete until we can accept all of ourselves – the good, the bad, and the ugly. Adversaries are mirrors showing us the parts of ourselves that we are unwilling to see. The suffering continues until we can see ourselves in the other person and the other person in ourselves. Once we realize that we are one with God's creation, the suffering stops, and our good starts to flow again.

Jesus was teaching his disciples how to end a negative cycle. If we keep resisting a person or an experience, it only gets worse. For example, many people hurt themselves worse by trying to avoid a fall. When they allow the fall to happen, it is never as bad as they thought. Allow all experiences to unfold, knowing that everything is in divine, right order, and that God's will for you is Absolute Good.

Day 31: Lust

"But I say unto you, that whosoever looks on a woman to lust after her has committed adultery with her already in his heart (Matthew 5:28)."

The Law and Prophets focused on adultery, the punishment of which was death. One of the Ten Commandments is "Thou shalt not commit adultery (Exodus 20:13)." In establishing his Kingdom, Jesus was not just concerned about the act of adultery, but he was concerned about the thoughts and feelings that led to adultery. Jesus understood that if we change the thoughts and feelings that lead to adultery, we can reduce or eliminate it. Jesus went beyond the surface action and saw that uncontrolled lust as what often leads to adultery.

Jesus got to the heart of the matter (lust) and not just the matter itself (adultery). Lust is an unlawful desire. An appropriate desire is to build rapport and a relationship with a single person to build a life together. Jesus taught his disciples to channel their sexual energy in the proper direction and to observe boundaries. Sexual violation happens to many people because their predators operate in lasciviousness, unbridled lust. Unbridled lust is a major cause of rape, incest, child molestation, adultery, and abuse of the elderly and mentally challenged.

Temperance is the ability to set limits and maintain boundaries around our thoughts, feelings, and behaviors. "He that has no rule over his own spirit is like a city that is broken down, and without walls (Proverbs 25:28)." A synonym for temperance is self-control. We cannot control others; we can only control ourselves as well as our passions. "He that rules his spirit is greater than he that taketh a city (Proverbs 16:32)." Jesus taught his disciples to focus on love instead of lust. When we love ourselves, we will not commit adultery because we realize that we deserve better. When we love others, we will not commit adultery because we do not desire to cause conflict in another person's relationship.

_____
_____
_____
_____
_____
_____

Day 32: Divorce

"But I say unto you, that whosoever shall put away his wife, saving for the cause of fornication, causes her to commit adultery: and whosoever shall marry her that is divorced commits adultery (Matthew 5:32)."

The Law and the Prophets allowed men to divorce women for any reason (Deuteronomy 24:1). If they found something displeasing about their wives, they put them out and gave them divorce papers. Society treated women like second class citizens. They had no rights and few privileges.

In establishing his Kingdom, Jesus was concerned about the treatment of women. Throughout his ministry, he liberated women. It was important to him that people did not consider women property. It was unacceptable to Jesus to discard women as if they were yesterday's garbage or used goods. He challenged his disciples to think about the impact that divorce had on women and their future relationships.

Jesus established adultery as a justifiable reason for divorce. In the Epistles, his disciples expanded divorce conditions to include abandonment (I Corinthians 7:15) and abuse (Ephesians 5:29). These 3 As (adultery, abandonment, abuse) empower us to see marriage as a divine institution that is not to be entered into or exited lightly. When we consider partnership, marriage, separation, or divorce, let us pray for God's guidance, knowing that God desires the highest and the best for all parties concerned.

Day 33: Vows

"*But I say unto you, swear not at all* (Matthew 5:34)."

The Law and the Prophets were profoundly serious about people keeping their word and being held accountable for what they said. They emphasized that a person must not make a vow, a promise, or a commitment unless they were sure that they would honor it no matter what. Like getting a loan from a bank or posting bail, people swore by collateral they were willing to lose if they did not keep their word.

In establishing his Kingdom, Jesus encouraged his disciples not to swear because they were only stewards. God is the Source and owner of all things. God calls us to be managers of what God entrusts into our hands. Just as the Word of God has power, our word must have power as well. When we say, "Yes," be sure that we mean yes. When we say "No," be confident in our no. When we are not clear about something, there is nothing wrong with saying, "Let me get back to you on that." When things change, communicate as soon as possible. This ensures you do not break your vow.

It is imperative that our account with the Universe is good so that when we speak to sickness, pain, disease, discomfort, and dysfunction, they move, and healing manifests (Matthew 21:21). We must be men and women of our word so that when we speak to chaos, contention, confusion, and competition, they dissipate, and love, joy, peace, harmony, unity, and equality reign. We must honor the words spoken out of our mouths so that when we speak to lack, limitation, poverty, and scarcity, they fade into nothingness and increase, abundance, overflow, and more than enough will come into fruition.

Day 34: Revenge

"But I say unto you, that you resist not evil: but whosoever shall smite you on your right cheek, turn to him the other also (Matthew 5:39)."

The Law and the Prophets focus on revenge, retaliation, retribution, and recompence. Jesus was establishing his Kingdom on ideals such as love, grace, mercy, and forgiveness. The Master's Manifesto was counterculture to the Old Testament's established protocols, especially the idea of turning the other cheek.

Revenge is taking matters into our own hands. When we seek revenge, it means we do not trust God to handle the situation appropriately. When we insist on retaliation, we demonstrate we do not believe in the **Kingdom Key of Sowing and Reaping** or karma (Galatians 6:6-10). When we focus our attention on retribution, we signal to the Universe to suspend grace and mercy so that we all can pay for everything that we have done. When we require recompence, we forget that God is our Source.

God encourages restoration over revenge. God emphasizes relationships instead of retaliation. God highlights rapport instead of retribution. God prioritizes reconciliation over recompense. We are always choosing between the Law and the Prophets and the Kingdom that Jesus established in his Manifesto.

___
___
___
___
___
___
___
___
___
___
___
___
___

Day 35: Love

"But I say unto you, love your enemies, bless them that curse you, do good to them that hate you, and pray for them which despitefully use you, and persecute you (Matthew 5:44)."

The word, Universe, means one word (uni=one, verse=word). According to the teachings of Jesus and his disciples, we fulfill all the scriptures in the Law and the Prophets in one word, love (Galatians 5:14). Jesus emphasized how easy it is to love those who are showing us love. It is natural to love those who love us. It is spiritual to love those who do not demonstrate love toward us.

God allows the sun to shine on the righteous and the unrighteous. God allows the rain to fall on the just as well as the unjust. Jesus used the Creator's example to show his disciples how to love. One way to measure our spiritual growth is by our ability to love those who hate us. We know that we are operating in the Christ consciousness when we can bless those who curse us. People see our holistic development when we do good to those who do evil things to us. Our divinity is evident when we choose to pray for those who despitefully use us instead of seeking revenge (Mathew 5:43-45).

Through his Manifesto, Jesus was establishing the Kingdom of Love. This teaching directly opposed the Jewish law of "An eye for an eye and a tooth for a tooth (Exodus 21:24)." Jesus challenged his disciples to function under a higher law, the Law of Love, where everyone was worthy of unconditional love.

My Mountaintop Experience – Divorce

I was always taught in Church that "God hates divorce. No matter what, stay together, stick together, and make it work." My second marriage, to my son's mom, ended in divorce, and I became a divorcee. My relationship with my ex-wife went through several changes. We were friends first, then lovers. Then we were co-parents and co-pastors. Only to become divorced and estranged. Finally, we were enemies and then cordial co-parents for the sake of our son.

For years, I carried shame around being divorced and wondered what was wrong with me. My wife and I were co-pastors of a growing congregation, and with all the anointing we had to preach, teach, and lead others, we were not able to make our marriage work. We were the picture-perfect family and conducted marriage workshops and couple's retreats, yet our marriage did not survive turbulent times. We went to spiritual direction, couple's therapy, and family counseling, and we still got a divorce.

I also felt guilty about being divorced because I had another marriage that did not last "until death do, we part." Since my first marriage to my twins' mom ended in death, the divorce felt like another failed marriage. During the pandemic, Bishop Hector and I worked as a team to sponsor Kingdom Conversations, a Monday Night virtual discussion with real people about relevant issues. The upcoming topic was Women in the Pulpit, and he felt that Elder Latonia Moss, my ex-wife, was an excellent panelist for the discussion. Latonia and I had not been on the same platform in over 16 years. He asked if I were comfortable sharing a virtual stage with her. Initially, I was not, but I heard the Spirit whisper, "Now is the time." I decided to have a mountaintop experience and ask for help. I used the Kingdom Spiritual Practice of Sharing to let people know that I was nervous and needed support. People from all over the country were praying with me.

Latonia and I were magic during the Kingdom Conversation. The synergy that we had as friends and co-pastors immediately returned as if there were no time and space between it. We continued our healing process through a two-part series, Life After Divorce. We shared our testimony with others about our divorce experience. We encouraged individuals to receive God's unconditional love, even though they had divorced. Our guidance empowered people, especially women, to rebuild their lives after divorce. What began as guilt and shame ended in overcoming and victory because we both took the high road and ascended to the mountain.

Your Mountaintop Experience

In the space below, describe a mountaintop experience that you had with separation/divorce or any of the other topics discussed this week: worship, adversaries, lust, vows, revenge, or love.

12 KEYS TO THE KINGDOM

LEAST & GREATEST
Matt. 5:19, 11:11, 13:32, Luke 7:27-29
Mustard Seed
Humility & Attitude

GOOD & EVIL
Matt. 6:21-23, 7:16-20, Jam. 3:9-12
Perception/View | Single Eye, Fruit
Singular vs. Duality

SHEEP & GOATS
Matthew 25:31-46
Parable of the Sheep & Goats
Service & Outreach

BINDING & LOOSING
Matthew 16:13-18
Position/Acceptance

WISE & FOOLISH
Matthew 25:1-13
Wise & Foolish Virgins
Preparation

FEW & MANY
Matthew 25:15-30
Parable of the Talents
Responsibility & Promotion

LIFE & DEATH
John 12:20-33, Prov. 18:21
Corn of wheat
Hope

SOWING & REAPING
Matthew 13:7-23
Various Soils
Decisions

LIGHT & DARKNESS
John 1:9, 3:19, 8:12, 9:5, 11:9, 12:46
Light
Truth/Revelation

FIRST & LAST
Matt. 20:7-17, 19:28-30
Laborers in the Vineyard
Order

LOST & FOUND
Luke 15
Lost Coin, Lost Son, Lost Sheep
Evangelism

OLD & NEW
Matthew 9:16-17
New Wine & Old Wineskins
Change

*[19] And I will give unto thee the **keys of the kingdom of heaven**: and whatsoever thou shalt bind on earth shall be bound in heaven: and whatsoever thou shalt loose on earth shall be loosed in heaven.* — Matthew 16:13-20

Week Six

Introduction - Intention

This week we will drill deeper into the intentions behind our actions. Not only must we do the right thing, but we must have the right motives. Motives matter. Jesus asked his disciples to do some soul-searching to ensure that they were doing spiritual practices from their hearts and not to impress others. Doing things from the heart is in and of itself rewarding. When we live from our *heart center*, we give, pray, forgive, and fast for the right reasons. When we live from spirit instead of our ego, our priorities and perceptions are in order, and we are worry-free.

This Week's Work at a Glance

Physical Heart

1. *Digestion*

    A Lot – Meatless Meals

    A Little – Chicken, turkey, seafood

    Avoid – Beef, lamb and pork

2. *Self-Care Strategy – Outward Appearance*

    Often, when we look our best, we do our best. Even if we are not feeling well, we start to feel better if we give some additional care to our appearance. Take care of yourself by giving yourself the necessary time for proper hygiene, and love yourself by making every effort to look your best.

3. *Collective Consciousness Prayer for Healing of Heart Aneurysms*

    Condition: Aortic aneurysms are an enlargement of the aorta, the main blood vessel that delivers blood to the body, at the abdomen's level.

    Prayer: We appreciate the experience and example of Jesus Christ on the cross by whose stripes we are already healed (I Peter 2:24). We are knowing the truth today that God heals us from aortic aneurysms. Our hearts are full of gratitude and appreciation that the healing has already happened. It is in the name and through the power and in the consciousness of Christ Jesus that it is so, so it is, and so we let it be.

Metaphysical Heart

4. *Heart Issue* – Hatred

   Hatred is prejudice toward or discrimination against people because they are different from you.

5. *Kingdom Practice for the Development of the Soul* – Visioning and Visualization

   A vision is a picture of the truth. It is an image of what God can do with, thru, and as you. Envision your oneness with all people regardless of the seeming differences of age, race, gender, culture, religion, orientation, socio-economic status, educational degrees, criminal background, or family dynamics. Imagine the seeming separation between you and them disappearing. Once you see the vision, hold it through visualization. Visualization is an "in your face" reminder of the vision and gives you a quick assessment of where you are in the process of the vision coming to pass. An example of visualization is a screen saver, a post on a mirror, or a reminder on your refrigerator.

Master's Manifesto

6. *Readings for the Week*

   Read the continuation of Jesus' Sermon on the Mount Matthew 6:1-32

7. *Matters that Matter*

   This week's topics: giving, prayer, forgiving, fasting, priorities, perceptions, and worry.

Day 36: Giving

"That your alms may be in secret: and your Father which sees in secret himself shall reward you openly (Matthew 6:4)."

Our giving is not to impress others. God entrusts us with finances to use at our discretion. Jesus calls his disciples to be good stewards of these finances and resources. We are to give from our hearts to anyone in need if we have the resources to do so.

Is every gift a tax credit? Jesus teaches his disciples to give in secret. Too often, people see their tithes and offerings as tax credits. We use envelopes and sophisticated tracking systems to ensure that we acknowledge and appreciate people for their giving. There is nothing wrong with these accounting procedures. Nevertheless, sometimes Spirit leads us to give without expecting to get anything in return, not even a thank you.

In the kingdom, we do not give to receive blessings or to avoid curses. As disciples of Christ, we realize that we are already blessed. We give because we understand the **Kingdom Key of Sowing and Reaping**. If we sow a little, then we will reap a little. If we sow plenty, then we will reap plenty. If we sow nothing, then we will reap nothing. When we give with the right motive and attitude, God rewards us for our giving. God rewards us openly and bountifully to show others how spiritual blessings become physical manifestations.

Day 37: Prayer

"When you pray, enter your closet, and when you have shut your door, pray to your Father which is in secret; and your Father who sees in secret shall reward you openly (Matthew 6:5)."

God honors sincere heartfelt prayers. We must be honest with God about where we are and what is going on in our lives. Ask God for guidance. Do not pray to be seen or heard by people. You are praying to God, and God will meet you at the point of your need. Prayer is the lifeline of every disciple.

Jesus gives two specific conditions that set the tone for effective prayer. First, "enter into your closet." The closet is that place of peace and tranquility. This closet can be both figurative and literal, whatever it takes to get you to focus. Second, "shut your door." Not only must we find that secret place, but once we enter, we must close the door of our minds to all the external clutter that hinders us.

Notice in the text that Jesus mentions the word "reward" twice. There is a connection between prayer and rewards. God will reward those who pray earnestly. The effectual fervent prayer of a righteous person avails much (James 5:16).

Day 38: Forgiveness

"For if you forgive people their trespasses, your heavenly Father will also forgive you: but if you forgive not people their trespasses, neither will your Father forgive your trespasses (Matthew 6:14-15)."

Prayer and forgiveness are coupled together, like prayer and fasting. Prayer is most effective when our conscience is clear, our hearts are pure, and our spirits are free. Forgiveness means to release and let go. When we forgive and ask for forgiveness, we clear the space for us to see and hear more clearly what Spirit is expressing.

We all need forgiveness. Ask God for forgiveness for anything that you have said, done, or thought that was not the highest and the best or the right and the perfect. God's forgiveness is always readily available to all of us. We must also forgive ourselves. The more are open to receive God's forgiveness, the easier it is to forgive ourselves and forgive others. When we hold things against people, we hold things against ourselves because we are all one. When we hold things against ourselves, we feel shame, guilt, and condemnation, blocking our ability to experience God's grace, mercy, and forgiveness.

Sometimes it also necessary for us to forgive God. Not that God has done anything wrong, but we have ideas about God that we need to release. We have held God responsible for various things in our lives, and we need to let them go. When we release and let go of all that is old, worn, unproductive, obsolete, and no longer serve us well, our communication with God, ourselves, and others only get better.

_____
_____
_____
_____
_____
_____
_____
_____
_____

Day 39: Fasting

"But you, when you fast, anoint your head, and wash your face; that you appear not unto men to fast (Matthew 6:17-18)."

In the Sermon on the Mount, Jesus also taught his disciples about fasting. He told them, *"Moreover when ye fast, be not, as the hypocrites, of a sad countenance: for they disfigure their faces, that they may appear unto men to fast. Verily I say unto you, they have their reward (Matthew 6:16)."* Therefore, whenever we prepare for a fast, we must examine our motives. We do not fast to impress others. Our motive for fasting is to draw us *closer* to Christ and not be an outward show to others. We do not need to make any public announcements at school, on our jobs, or in our communities about the fact that we are fasting. We only need to share our fasting with a person or a group if we feel that it might alleviate confusion or entice them to join us in the spiritual practice by sharing it with them.

At the start of a corporate fast, we anoint the participants with oil and lay hands on them so that the anointing of God will rest upon them. The anointing is the enablement of the Holy Spirit to do a specific task. Like oil, the anointing makes things easier. The anointing empowers us to do what it takes to be successful in fasting endeavors.

Jesus taught his disciples the value and rewards of fasting. *"That you appear not unto men to fast, but unto your Father which is in secret: and your Father, which sees in secret, shall reward thee openly (Matthew 6:18)."* Jesus felt that fasting was valuable enough to teach about it. He also spoke of the reward in fasting. If we follow the proper procedures for fasting, then we receive a reward. God will bless our efforts. The Lord will release natural and spiritual blessings in our lives due to observing this spiritual practice.

_____

_____

_____

_____

_____

_____

_____

_____

Day 40: Priorities

"For where your treasure is, there will your heart be also (Matthew 6:21)."

In the Law and the Prophets, people gave tithes and offerings to be blessed. If they did not pay their tithes and offerings, they were considered cursed (Malachi 3:8-10). It was not a matter of the heart. Giving was more of an obligation like a bill or a tax that required payment to avoid consequences.

Treasure often represents money. It also refers to whatever we value. Jesus connected giving with the heart and saw it as a matter of priorities. We can tell what is important to us by how we spend our time and our money. It is clear what our priorities are by what we do first and where we direct our attention.

God is the Source of our time, our talents, and our treasure. They all belong to God, and we are stewards or managers of the resources that God gives us. When we give God the first part of our day and are conscious of spending quality time with God through our Kingdom Practices for the Development of the Soul, we demonstrate our love for God. Let us be intentional about utilizing our talents to build God's Kingdom through volunteer efforts and community service. When we sow funds to the spiritual community that feeds us, we express our appreciation for the growth that we are experiencing and our desire to develop our Christ consciousness even more.

Day 41: Perception/Focus

"The light of the body is the eye: if therefore your eye is single, your whole body shall be full of light (Matthew 6:22)."

Dualism is at the root of many Christians' relationships with God. Dualism is the belief that two opposing gods are equal in power and at war with one another. It is essential in our prayers that we pray and talk to God instead of interrupting our conversation with God to bind the devil. Many see everything good as coming from Jehovah (the good god) and everything evil from the Satan (the evil god).

Jesus invited his disciples to see life from the single eye instead of a dualistic perspective. Everything that happens in our lives comes from God, whether we label it good or evil. Through a single-lens, it is all good because it is all God. There are lessons and blessings. A lesson is the good that is not apparent. A blessing is the good that is apparent.

Let us worship the one God, the Good Omnipotence, as our Source. Let us take responsibility for our way of being, seeing, thinking, speaking, and behaving instead of blaming the devil as a scapegoat. When we make poor choices, let us accept and learn from them instead of saying the "devil made me do it." Neither Satan, the devil, nor demons have power over us. Jesus said, "Behold, I give you power to tread on serpents and scorpions and over all the power of the enemy (Luke 10:19)." As God's beloved offspring, it is time for us to rise and use the power that Christ delegated to us and stop using the devil as an excuse for our spiritual immaturity.

Day 42: Worry

"Therefore, take no thought, saying, what shall we eat? or, what shall we drink? or, Wherewithal shall we be clothed (Matthew 6:31) *?"*

The opposite of love is fear. When we operate in love, we do not need to fear. "Perfect love casts out all fear (I John 4:18)." The opposite of faith is doubt. When we operate in faith, we bring the good that already exists from the invisible to the visible, releasing doubt. "For verily I say unto you, that whosoever shall say unto this mountain, be removed, and be cast into the sea; and shall not doubt in his heart but shall believe that those things which he says shall come to pass; he shall have whatsoever he says (Mark 11:23)." The opposite of worry is hope. When we remember the truth that all is well, worry fades away, and we live in hope. "This I recall to my mind; therefore, have I hope (Lamentations 3:21)."

Jesus taught his disciples to hope for the future instead of worrying about the future. God did not design us to carry stress from yesterday into today. God did not create us to take worry about tomorrow into today. Our bodies and our minds cannot handle the pressure of yesterday, today, and tomorrow at one time.

When we attempt to function in the past, the present, and the future simultaneously, our bodies manifest disease, dysfunction, and discomfort, and our minds demonstrate chaos, confusion, and contention. There is nothing wrong with planning, having goals, and aspirations if we remain open and flexible to the guidance of Spirit. The best way to live is to release the past, live in the present moment experiencing all presents that God has for us right here and right now, and be flexible about our future.

My Mountaintop Experience: Worry

As the Presiding Prelate of the Church of the Everlasting Kingdom, the Spiritual Leader of Today's Church Tampa Bay, the President of the Gathering of Pastors, and the President of Interfaith Tampa Bay, I had to address the COVID-19 pandemic and its impact on these organizations. I ascended to the mountaintop for words that could transcend fear, doubt, and worry. The Holy Spirit gave me the following words:

During this Lenten Season, the spread of the Coronavirus gained global attention. We all desire health, not only for ourselves but also for our family, friends, and brothers and sisters of the Universe. I know that it can be challenging to stand on the Kingdom Principles when the appearances of sickness, pain, disease, discomfort, and dysfunction seem predominant in the news media and are often the topic of conversations.

I believe in you, and I know that you have what it takes within you to be a calm, loving, peaceful presence for all those who are afraid and stressed. "Greater is he (God) that is within you than he that is in the world (I John 4:4)." I see our local assemblies, ministries, and businesses as places of refuge where people can pray and experience the peace of God, which passes all understanding (Philippians 4:7). I pray that we offer people hope and a divine perspective of a higher purpose and a bigger plan than what we experience with our natural senses.

While we continue to take the precautions of handwashing, sanitizing areas, and building our immune systems, let us remember that physical manifestations are only signs of deeper global issues that need healing. Things come up and out to be healed. God has brought us through various epidemics and pandemics in the past. As God brings us through this one, let us keep our minds stayed on him (God) so that we can operate in perfect peace despite the chaos, confusion, and unrest that is all around us (Isaiah 26:3).

Join me in consciousness as I hold the vision of the virus's containment instead of its spread. Envision with me a vaccine for the virus instead of more people transitioning due to the virus. Let us wrap the Coronavirus in light and love knowing that it has served its purpose so it can now return to the nothingness from which it came.

It is no accident that this is happening during the Lenten Season, where people are focused on prayer and fasting. During this time of consecration, find comfort and strength in the **Kingdom Principle of Divine Protection:**

There is a Divine Protection in the Universe. We honor, revere, and respect God; therefore, the angels of the Lord encamp around us. There is a hedge of protection around us. Anything that gets through that hedge of protection God meant for God's glory and our highest good."

Your Mountaintop Experience

In the space provided below, write about your own mountaintop experience with worry or any of the other topics addressed this week: giving, prayer, forgiving, fasting, priorities, or perception.

Week 7

Introduction – The Kingdom of God

"But seek first the kingdom of God and his righteousness, and all these things shall be added unto you (Matthew 6:33)."

Three systems operate on the earth: the World, the Church, and the Kingdom. The World focuses on the physical, the temporal, the earthly, and the external. The worldly realm leaves God out. The Church is the midpoint between the World and the Kingdom. The Kingdom is a system where God, the Spirit of Absolute Good, is in the center.

The word kingdom appears in the Bible over 350 times. Most references to kingdom in the Old Testament refer to natural kingdoms. Most references in the New Testament refer to the Kingdom of God.

There are four major biblical definitions of the Kingdom. First, the Kingdom is the place where the King rules and reigns (Luke 17:20-21). Secondly, Kingdom is when God's will in heaven is being done on the earth (Matthew 6:10). Thirdly, Kingdom is an internal system, a form of government, a way of being, seeing, thinking, speaking, and behaving in which God is the center (Matthew 6:33). Finally, The Kingdom of God is righteousness, peace, and joy in the Holy Ghost (Romans 14:17). Jesus is the King of the Kingdom. He established the Kingdom to shift the focus to the spiritual, the everlasting, the heavenly, and the internal.

This Week's Work at a Glance

Physical Heart

1. *Digestion*

A Lot – Water, fruit, vegetables, nuts, lentils, beans

A Little – Flat Bread and veggie noodles

Avoid – Pizza and pasta

2. *Self-Care Strategy* – Recreation

God desires us to live holistically healthy, balanced, and well-rounded lives. We must have fun and take time for vacations, holidays, hobbies, and our favorite pastimes.

3. *Collective Consciousness Prayer* for the Healing of Coronary Artery Disease

Condition: Coronary Artery Disease occurs when bad cholesterol and plaque clog the arteries and cause chest pains and shortness of breath.

Prayer: We let go of all unhealthy habits associated with coronary artery disease along with the signs and symptoms of chest pains and shortness of breath. Just as Jesus, the living Word, went to various places preaching the Gospel of the Kingdom and healing every disease among the people, we allow that same healing word and virtue to heal us from coronary artery disease (Matthew 9:35). It is in the name and through the power and in the consciousness of Christ Jesus that it is so, so it is, and so we let it be.

Metaphysical Heart

4. *Heart Issue* – Slander

Slander is wanting to destroy someone's reputation by spreading rumors or breaking confidentiality due to hurt feelings.

5. *Kingdom Practice for the Development of the Soul* - Fellowship

Spending time with like-minded people who are doing the things you desire to do or that you enjoy is beneficial. Fellowship leads to connections that can enhance your health, harmonious relationships, and wealth. Building genuine rapport and establishing authentic relationships with other positive people who may not be aware of their spiritual identity leads them to a deeper connection with the Divine. As you lift the universe's vibration and the planet's energy through fellowship, you have no desire to bring others down through slander.

Master's Manifesto

6. *Readings for the Week*

    Read the conclusion of Jesus' Sermon on the Mount Matthew 6:33-7:27

7. *Matters that Matter*

    This week's topics: Judging, Discernment, Asking/Seeking/Knocking, The Golden Rule, The Way, The Fruit, and The Solid Foundation.

Day 43: Judging

"Judge not, that you be not judged (Matthew 7:1)."

Jesus, the Wayshower, established a Kingdom of Love. When the Jewish leaders brought the woman caught in the act of adultery, Jesus refused to operate according to the old Law of Moses, which required death by stoning (John 8:1-12). He operated according to a new higher law, the law of love (Matthew 22:34-40). Jesus was a physical demonstration of the love of God by being a judgment-free zone for this woman in a challenging position. He was primarily interested in her learning and growing from the experience. His love reigned supreme so much so that the woman's accusers had no choice but to love her or leave the situation.

The same love of God inside of Jesus, as our Master Teacher, is inside you. In every situation, you have a choice to manifest love or to be judgmental. Give love and compassion to yourself. As you give love and compassion to yourself, you will discover more opportunities to give love and compassion to others.

Under the old Law, there was guilt, shame, and condemnation. In the Kingdom that Jesus established, there is no guilt, shame, and condemnation, only love (Romans 8:1). Jesus knew that his mission was not to judge others, and he taught his disciples not to judge either. "God did not send his Son into the world to condemn the world but that the world through him might be saved (John 3:17)." Do not judge people because they are following their journey to wholeness. Only God has the authority to judge (Romans 14:4). You do not know enough about people or their path to make an assessment (Matthew 7:1-2). All you can do is love them and encourage them to continue their voyage.

Day 44: Discernment

"Give not that which is holy unto the dogs, neither cast ye your pearls before swine, lest they trample them under their feet, and turn again and rend you (Matthew 7:6)."

Jesus did not mince words in his Manifesto to his disciples. He used strong language and compared people to dogs and swine. Through the example of our Wayshower, we realize that sometimes we must be stern and send a pungent message to get our audience's attention.

As a Master Teacher, he guided his disciples to have discernment about their value. It is imperative that we know our worth and see the gifts that we have to offer to the earth as holy. Each of us must assign the value of pearls to the knowledge, wisdom, and understanding that we gained through education and experience.

Only you can determine who the dogs and pigs are in your life. Just because they may appear as a dog to you does not mean that they are dogs. Just because they appear as swine to you does not mean that they are pigs. They are God's beloved offspring, just like you. It just means that what you have is not for them, and what they have is not for you. They will discover that which is holy for them. They will find where their pearls are. Do not try to force a fit. Let it flow. We live in an abundant universe. People are looking for you, the authentic you, and what you have to offer.

_____
_____
_____
_____
_____
_____
_____
_____
_____
_____
_____
_____

Day 45: Asking, Seeking, and Knocking

"For every one that asks receives; and he that seeks finds and to him that knocks it shall be opened (Matthew 7:8)."

In a Prayer & Healing Service, Minister Gina Folk, our Director of Teaching, brought to my attention that ask, seek and knock form an acronym for prayer—A.S.K. Asking in prayer is more than making a request. Verbalizing our needs and desires is just the beginning of the A.S.K.

The A.S.K. continues with us seeking. Seeking is taking action about what we are praying for and going after it with our whole hearts. "Faith without works is dead (James 2:20)." The final dimension of the A.S.K. is knocking. Knocking is perseverance (Ephesians 6:18). Like the widow and the unjust judge, it means that we do not give up until we see the manifestation of our prayers (Luke 18:1-8).

The Kingdom principles, practices, and promises that Jesus, our Wayshower, taught his disciples are universal and can work for anyone who utilizes them. Jesus, the Master Teacher, emphasized that prayer, the A.S.K., is for everyone. God answers the prayers of anyone who will ask, seek and knock.

Day 46: The Golden Rule

"Therefore, all things whatsoever ye that men would do to you, do ye even so to them: for this is the law and the prophets (Matthew 7:12)."

I remember in Sunday School learning the Golden Rule, "do unto others as you would have them do unto you." Many of us have heard this simple principle, but how many of us really practice it? According to this principle, we treat people how we desire others to treat us, not how they treat us. The critical distinction in this powerful teaching is "desired versus actual" treatment.

We all desire the same treatment, acceptance. We all need to be loved and respected for who we are. Many people encourage us to "teach tolerance." However, do people want to be tolerated? No. They desire to be accepted. God has not called us to tolerate people. God called us to love people. Love is unconditional acceptance. Love and respect are not something people have to earn; they are something we owe everyone. We owe it to people to love them (Romans 13:8). They deserve respect because God made them in the image and likeness of God, just like us (Genesis 1:26-28).

As we continue to grow in our discipleship, we reach the highest form of love, celebration. Tolerance develops into acceptance, and acceptance evolves into celebration. People desire celebration of their existence. They naturally gravitate to people and places where they feel celebrated. Let us celebrate our unity and our uniqueness. Let us celebrate our divinity and our diversity. They are not in conflict with one another. They complement one another.

Day 47: The Way

"Because strait is the gate, and narrow is the way, which leads unto life, and few there be that find it (Matthew 7:14)."

Jesus, the Master Teacher, taught his disciples about the narrow way and the broad way (Matthew 7:13). The broad way represents our failed attempts to find someone or something outside of ourselves to make us whole. The broad way is a destructive path that keeps us searching but never satisfies. The narrow way is the realization that everything we need and desire is inside us because God is inside us. Things work from the "inside out," not the "outside-in."

Our faith is the calm assurance that God meets all our needs, answers all our prayers, opens all our doors, and gives us the good desires of our heart (II Peter 1:3). Therefore, we can hold in our minds the picture of our good or something better. Our Kingdom Practices for the Development of our Soul cause us to remember the truth that "All is well all the time with everybody everywhere!"

Jesus, our Wayshower, said, "I AM the way, the truth and the life no man comes to the Father but by me (John 14:6)." As human beings, our souls question and wonder how our good will unfold. Jesus, our Wayshower, gave us the answer when he said, "I AM the way." The I AM is the way for all our good to manifest. When we meditate and focus on the words, "I AM," we bring the good God intended for us into expression. When we speak, "I AM," we demonstrate our divinity. When we sing, "I AM," all things become possible. I AM is the Way! There is no other way to obtain and maintain our highest good without the actualization of the I AM!

Day 48: Fruit

"Wherefore by their fruits, ye shall know them (Matthew 7:20)."

The Fruit of the Spirit reveals God's nature and character. The Fruit of the Spirit is the evidence of the Holy Spirit in the life of a disciple. Evidence is proof that no one can discredit. We can not mimic love. How we manifest love is a direct correlation to our relationship with God. When we are in right relationship with God, love flows from us just as freely as our breath. When we are not in right relationship with God, we struggle to love ourselves and others.

Jesus gave his disciples a character badge by which all people could recognize them as his followers. He said in John 13:35, "by this shall all men know that you are my disciples if you have love one for another." Love is the badge of discipleship. All other demonstrations and manifestations are temporary (I Corinthians 13:8). The badge is not prophecies because they will fail. The badge is not speaking in other tongues because it ceases. The badge is not knowledge because it will pass away. The badge is love. Only love will last forever.

Love is the greatest gift of all (I Corinthians 13:1-4). Without love, speaking in tongues is just making noise. Without love, faith and prophecy mean nothing. No matter how much knowledge we have, without love, we are nothing. Jesus Christ manifested God's love to all people. Love is the only true virtue that identifies us as his disciples; anything else is a fake id.

Day 49: Solid Foundation

"Therefore, whosoever heareth these sayings of mine, and doeth them; I will liken him unto a wise man, which built his house upon a rock (Matthew 7:24)."

Jesus taught his disciples the importance of having a solid foundation for their lives. Hearing the Kingdom principles and the practices are like building your life on sand. Sand is a substance, but it is not durable. Hearing the Kingdom principles and practices and making them a part of your daily life builds your house on a rock. A rock is a solid foundation.

The house built on sand and the house built on the rock both had the same rain, wind, and storm events, but they had different results. Our relationship with God is not an exemption certificate from life's trials. We fall when we do not live the truth that we know. What keeps us standing is applying the principles and practices to every aspect of our lives.

Jesus said, "In this world, you will have tribulation. Let not your heart be troubled. I have overcome the world (John 16:33)." As he gets to the end of his Manifesto, he urges his disciples to practice all that he taught them. Like taking a course, there will be a test to show you what you have learned, what you need to re-learn, and what you need to unlearn. If you continue to follow Jesus' example, you can overcome any external conditional through the power that is within you (I John 4:4).

My Mountaintop Experience – The Golden Rule

When I moved to St. Petersburg, Florida, I desired to establish rapport and build relationships with people in my new hometown. One of my clergy colleagues invited me to go to an interfaith breakfast. Up until this point, I had only been to interdenominational events with other Christians. I never attended an interfaith gathering in Baltimore or any of my travels throughout the United States and abroad. I felt hesitant and fearful about stepping outside of my comfort zone and trying something new. I decided to use my Kingdom Spiritual Practice of Scripture, Denials, and Affirmations to help me navigate through the fear of the unknown.

Scripture – "God has not given us the spirit of fear but of power, love and a sound mind (II Timothy 1:7)."

Denial – My past experiences do not define me.

Affirmation – I AM open and receptive to divine unlimited ideas.

The topic of discussion at my first breakfast for the St. Petersburg Interfaith Association was the Golden Rule. People were there from different faith traditions explaining how the Golden Rule was expressed and practiced in their spiritual communities. The Bahai Faith members stated, "Choose thou for thy neighbor that which thou choosest for thyself." The Jews aligned with Christians and espoused "Love thy neighbor as thyself." The Muslims exclaimed, "None of you truly believes until he wishes for his brother what he wishes for himself." Hinduism asserted, "Do not to others what ye do not wish done to yourself; and wish for others too what ye desire and long for, for yourself." Buddhism acknowledged, "Make thine own self the measure of the others, and so abstain from causing hurt to them."

Although the words were different, the message was the same. We are all here to love one another and treat people how we desire them to treat us. It was clear that we all desire the same thing; to be loved, respected, and accepted. I left the breakfast on the mountaintop. I learned that truth is universal and that love is not limited to Christianity. Truth transcends religion, and love surpasses culture. Since that first breakfast, I missed very few interfaith meetings and events. Eventually, the group changed its name to Interfaith Tampa Bay, and I became the secretary and the chaplain. Currently, I AM honored to serve as the president of this organization.

Your Mountaintop Experience

In the space below, describe a mountaintop experience that you had with this topic of the Golden Rule or any of the other topics discussed this week: Judging, Discernment, Asking/Seeking/Knocking, The Way, The Fruit, and The Solid Foundation.

Week Seven

Conclusion

Living in Power and Authority

"And it came to pass when Jesus had ended these sayings; the people were astonished at his doctrine: for he taught them as one having authority, and not as the scribes (Matthew 7:28-29)."

When Jesus finished sharing his Manifesto on Matters that Mattered, people were shocked by his boldness to share his Kingdom message. Today, God calls us to walk in that same power and authority. It is more than just saying "in the name of Jesus" at the end of prayer (John 16:22-27). Continuing the Kingdom Consciousness that Jesus operated in is understanding that we have that same power and authority and can function as if we were him. We can live with that same confidence and assurance that God will support us in the same way that God supported Jesus. This Manifesto is like a signed document giving us power of attorney to function on Jesus' behalf. We have a blank check with his signature. It's now up to us to take the Kingdom message to the next dimension and apply it to this generation.

Now that we have studied the Master's Manifesto on Matters that Matter, it is up to us to continue to live it. As current day disciples of Jesus Christ, we can continue his mission. Now that Jesus is no longer here in a physical form and the original disciples have transitioned, it is up to us to pick up the baton and carry on the race. Let us be who Jesus was, say what Jesus said, and do what Jesus did and even greater works (John 14:12).

The affirmation below will help you continue your Consciousness Journey.

Affirm daily:

Everything that Jesus Christ was, I AM.

I AM Savior.

I AM Christ.

I AM lord.

I AM king.

I AM god.

Everything that Jesus Christ said about himself, I can say about myself.

I AM the bread of life.

I AM the living water.

I AM the light of the world.

I AM the salt of the earth.

I AM the way.

I AM the truth.

I AM the life.

I AM the door.

I AM the true vine.

I AM the Good Shepherd.

I AM the resurrection and the life.

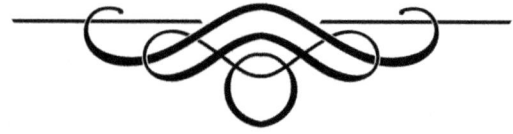

Week Seven

**Everything that Jesus Christ did,
I can do and even greater works (John 14:12).**

I can preach with power.

I can teach with authority.

I can heal the sick.

I can raise the dead.

I can cast out devils, which are negative influences.

I can change the atmosphere.

I can empower the blind to see.

I can empower the deaf to hear.

I can empower the dumb to speak.

I can empower the lame to walk.

I can cleanse lepers, those with seemingly incurable diseases.

I can forgive sins.

I can feed the multitudes naturally and spiritually.

I can turn water into wine.

I can walk on water.

I can speak to the elements of nature, and they obey my voice.

The truth is I can do all things through Christ who strengthens me (Philippians 4:13).

It is so, and so it is, and so I let it be.

About the Author

Dr. Doral R. Pulley celebrates over 40 years in ministry. He has traveled throughout the United States and to other countries preaching the Kingdom message, teaching Kingdom principles, leading entities and developing people. He has also written 5 books and 13 devotional journals.

Dr. Pulley holds a Bachelor of Arts degree in Religious Studies and Theology from Morgan State University (1992), a Master of Science degree in Pastoral Counseling from Loyola University (1996), and a Doctorate in Ministry from Graduate Theological Foundation (2010). He is also a certified Mental Health Professional by the National Board of Professional Counselors (1998).

Dr. Pulley is the Presiding Prelate of the Church of the Everlasting Kingdom, Inc. (2003) and the founding president of Alpha Nu Omega Fraternity, Inc (1998). He is the president of the two community organizations: The Gathering of Pastors (2018) and Interfaith Tampa Bay (2019).

Dr. Pulley is the Establishmentarian and Spiritual Leader of Today's Church Tampa Bay, one church with two locations in Florida Tampa (2017) and St. Petersburg (2019). Under his leadership, this local assembly continues to experience spiritual, numerical, financial and physical growth.

Dr. Pulley is the father of twin daughters: Brittney and Courtney, one son, D. Reginald, II and the proud grandfather of Tyler Jade.

doctorpulley.com

Resources

APPENDIX

The "I AM" Admonitions
(excerpted from the 2020 COTEK Ordinal)

Candidate: I AM the bread of life. People can feed off of my life. I AM the living water. People can drink from my divine substance.

Consecrator: Who are you?

Candidate: I AM the light of the world. I shine even in dark places and people come to the light.

Consecrator: Who are you?

Candidate: I AM the resurrection and the life. I give life to all that come in contact with me.

Consecrator: Who are you?

Candidate: I AM the way, the truth and the life. People come to the Father by me.

Consecrator: How well do you know Him?

Candidate: He is the Lord of my life. He is the Lord of lords. I accept the responsibility of being a lord in the earth.

Consecrator: How well do you know Him?

Candidate: He is the King of kings. I AM a king in the earth and I rule and reign in my domain.

Consecrator: How well do you know Him?

Candidate: He is the God of gods. I AM God manifested in the flesh. I AM a god in the earth to-day.

www.ingramcontent.com/pod-product-compliance
Lightning Source LLC
Chambersburg PA
CBHW071721040426
42446CB00011B/2161